GOD WILL MAKE A WAY

PERSONAL DISCOVERY GUIDE

DR. HENRY CLOUD
DR. JOHN TOWNSEND

GOD
WILL MAKE
A WAY

PERSONAL
DISCOVERY GUIDE

INTEGRITY®
PUBLISHERS

Nashville

Editor: Lisa Guest
Cover Design: David Uttley, UDG | DesignWorks
Interior Design: Susan Browne Design

ISBN 1-59145-079-9
ISBN 1-59145-378-X (New Cover)

Printed in United States of America
05 06 07 08 09 DPS 9 8 7 6 5 4 3 2 1

CONTENTS

WE ALL NEED A WAY

I (Henry) was almost four years old when the pain began, and the pain did not go away for months. My parents were people of faith, having learned in their own journey that, when your back is up against the wall and you pray and seek his help, God will make a way through the trial. So it was not unusual for them to lean on God for help in a tough time.

My parents prayed every day even though their emotions were in tumult. They did not understand why a happy, healthy little boy would suddenly be looking at the prospect of losing a normal life. What had they, or I, done to deserve this? Yet as they prayed, they felt a certain steadiness inside, despite the fear.

1. *When, if ever, have you prayed more out of the knowledge that it was the right thing to do rather than a passion for, or even confidence in, prayer?*

2. *For what present situation do you need to pray despite tumultuous emotions? Who can pray for you and with you?*

My mother and a friend had taken me to another doctor's visit. As we sat in the waiting room and time passed, my mother felt her fear growing. The doctor was not showing, and she just did not know what to expect. Still we waited . . . and waited. Then it happened. Suddenly my mother felt something inside of her, almost as if a voice said, *Take him to New Orleans.* That meant only one thing to my mother. It meant that she should take me to Oschner's Clinic, the famous training hospital in New Orleans. My mother knew that God must be making a way for us there. How did she convince my dad, a no-nonsense businessman? I do not know, but the three of us set off for New Orleans—going on pure faith.

3. *As you wait for God to guide you in the situations you have referred to, what are you doing to listen for him?*

4. *What step of faith might God be asking you to take? What hesitation, if any, do you have—and what will you do to overcome it? Who will you ask to hold you accountable for taking this step of faith?*

When we checked in at Oschner's Clinic, we were randomly assigned to a new doctor on their staff, Mary Sherman. After x-rays were taken, Dr. Sherman told us that she had diagnosed what was wrong with me. I had necrosis—soft tissue that was dying—in my hip joint. Although this rare condition was serious if not properly treated, she knew exactly what to do. I would have to be in a wheelchair and on crutches with leg braces, but within a year or two I would be back to normal. How did she know?

Dr. Sherman had recently been trained in her residency under the two doctors in the U.S. who had extensive experience with this particular rare disease. This made her one of only a few doctors, at that time, who knew how to diagnose my disease this early and provide the necessary treatment. If God had not intervened and impressed my mother to take me to New Orleans, it is unlikely we would have found a cure in time. He had supernaturally led her to the one doctor who could help.

5. *When has God supernaturally intervened in your life or the life of someone you know?*

6. *If you're unable to identify a specific situation, ask God to give you eyes to see his active presence in your life, either today, looking back, or both.*

My mother and father discovered that God continued to make a way during the next few years, as they learned how to deal with a disabled child. Every step of the way, God provided for us. If you ask my parents today, they will tell you that all eighty-seven years of their lives have been just like that as well. No matter what the crisis, God has made a way.

The Way Is Not Always As Easy to See *(4*)*

(* The number after each subhead refers to the page in the God Will Make a Way *book [Integrity, 2002] so that you can find a more complete discussion of the topic if you're interested.)*

Life's crises do not always turn out as well as mine did. Every one of us has times when we lose, and we hurt, and we find ourselves asking, "Where is God in all this?" Often, it's not easy to see where God is when the road gets hard.

7.   *Why are you asking right now (if you are), "Where is God in all this?"*

8.   *What and/or who might help you see where God is?*

What countless stories like mine tell us is that there are many times and many surprising ways that God shows up and changes even the most hopeless situations. One of the most powerful, though difficult, lessons we all need to learn on our spiritual pilgrimage is that even when bad things happen and we do not understand why, we can trust God to be present and working on our behalf.

9. *When has God surprised you and shown up in a hopeless situation? Be specific —and be encouraged!*

10. *What "bad things" are touching your life right now? Why can you "trust God to be present and working on [your] behalf"?*

Consider the biblical account of Job. His friends gave him answer after answer for the tragedies in his life. But God's response was not really an answer at all; it was an encounter. God met Job face to face. Most people will tell you that in the midst of the most unspeakable suffering, they don't want an explanation; they want your presence. The ultimate answer, then, to the problem of pain is a person. It's God himself. And *God still shows up in very powerful ways.* God makes a way even through death and suffering by revealing his presence. We never know when, where, or how he is going to show up, but he will.

11. *When has someone's presence, rather than his or her words, been a source of comfort to you? Be specific and use a recent example if possible.*

12. *Explain, if you're able, how God revealed his presence to you and/or loved and encouraged you through that person.*

13. *In what current situation would the presence of a friend mean more than any words he or she might speak? Why is presence so important?*

At times in my own life, God has made a way for me by sending just the right people—the ones who could tell me the next step to take in finding him or who could help me work through some major losses and pain in my life. When I reached out to God for help, he provided these people. And they were able to bring to me and teach me exactly what I needed at that time. The key, I have learned, is to reach out to God for help.

14. *What (sometimes or even often) keeps you from reaching out to God for help?*

15. *What might make such reaching out easier or more automatic and natural for you?*

When we reach out to God for help, God has some pretty surprising ways of getting us the help we need—even when things look really bleak. And even when the problem is of our own making.

Many Feel Helpless and Hopeless (7)

Recently John and I received a call during our daily radio show from Marian, a middle-class career woman who, in a not-so-smart moment, had "just once" tried crack cocaine. The drug had instantly gripped her. Addicted, helpless, hopeless, and feeling terribly guilty, Marian decided to turn to God. She had been going to church, thinking that finding God meant making a commitment to being good, stopping the drug use, and attending church. I interrupted her and explained that she was not finding God, but religion instead.

16. *Explain in your own words the difference between finding God and finding religion.*

Religion is about trying to be better people than we are and using "God language" and even a "God address"—like a church—in which to do it. But God does not depend on our willpower and commitment to transform a hopeless situation. God's way is through grace—that is, by *his providing what we cannot provide for ourselves.*

17. *When did you find God, not just religion?*

18. *What compassion, support, understanding, love, and/or power have you experienced since finding God? Give a few examples.*

19. *If you haven't found God, what is keeping you from seeking him?*

God provided a way for Marian through his people. First, John and I knew of the perfect drug rehabilitation center for her. Second, people from all over the country called to say they felt as if they were supposed to pay for Marian to get treatment. When it became apparent that she was going to come up $5,400 short, a woman called who wanted to give God a tithe on an inheritance she'd received a few years before. The inheritance was $54,000, and she wanted to give $5,400. God had made a way for Marian, who could see no way to get the help she desperately needed.

20. *When has God made a way for you (or someone you know)?*

21. *In what current situation do you want to trust God to make a way for you? (Remember the father's wonderful prayer from Mark 9:24—"I do believe; help me overcome my unbelief!" Make that prayer your own.)*

As God demonstrated with Marian, he can find a way for you wherever you might be. Little did that woman know that her call from the Midwest, to a radio station in California, would land her in a treatment center in Arizona paid for by people from several other states. God is never limited in how he can make a way or what that way might look like.

But I'm Not an Addict, and I Haven't Lost Anyone *(9)*

You may be wondering how God will make a way if you don't feel as if you have lost your way. The fact is, if you think that your life is perfect and cannot get any better, then you are right—you don't need any help. You have already arrived at heaven. I think that is great. Unusual, but great.

In reality, I've never seen a person who felt that his or her life was perfect. But even if you believe you have arrived, then God can *still* make a way for you to give to others. Ask him today whom he can send you to, and, believe me, he will give you a mission.

Chances are that you have not reached a place in life where you are beyond the need for God's help and grace. Chances are that you are a normal person, living a reasonably normal life. So let's talk about normal.

Most normal people often feel there is something missing in their lives. There is a distance between where they are and where they want to be. We call that the "gap." This longing usually expresses itself in one or more areas of your life.

+ **You want your relationships to be closer.**

22. *What relationship(s) in your life could be better, closer, and more intimate?*

✦ **You want to be in control of your life.**

23. *What gap is there between where you are in life and where you want to be? Consider your personal goals, the way you think and act, the way you feel, and your accomplishments. Are you living up to your potential and/or fulfilling your dreams? Who will hold you accountable to working toward those dreams and encourage you along the way?*

✦ **You want to satisfy your spiritual hunger.**

24. *Are you experiencing a gap between yourself and God? Do you want to be more passionate about your faith?*

However your longing expresses itself—relationally, personally, or spiritually—if you are in the gap, feeling stuck between your disappointing circumstances and your hopes and dreams for life, we have good news: God will make a way for you if you call on him. But here is where things sometimes get difficult. Most people cannot see God's way for them because they have difficulty believing there is a way.

EXERCISE FAITH IN THE WAY *(11)*

The main obstacle to finding God's way through the crises and gaps of life is failing to believe a way exists. Don Moen's touching lyric promises, "God will make a way where there seems to be no way." But how do we find that way? How can we transcend the trials and tragedies of life? It starts by believing God indeed will make a way. It's a matter of embracing and exercising faith in God.

Most of us don't have difficulty simply believing in God. But for some reason we are reticent when it comes to really trusting God. We think, *Will he come through for me? Can I depend on him? Will he make a way for me?*

25. *Which area(s) of your life do you find hard to trust to God? Why?*

26. *What evidence of God's trustworthiness and ability to handle the challenges, trials, and tragedies of your life have you witnessed (in your life or someone else's)?*

Trust is how we access God's way for us. Trust is acting on your belief that God will make a way. Trust is both an *attitude* and an *action*. Your first small step must be followed by another, and another, until you realize that God has indeed made a way for you to know him personally. The more you act on your faith in God, the more you will see of his way for you.

27. *"Trust is both an attitude and an action." What part of this statement do you find especially challenging or intriguing?*

28. *What will you do to test this assertion? What small step of faith will you take this week?*

When God makes a way for you through your trials and your everyday problems, it is an active, not passive, process. God is active on your behalf even when you cannot see it. And he calls you to be active also. God will do what only he can do, and your job is to do what you can do. That's when faith really shines.

29. *Marian could not kick her crack habit or find the money for treatment. God had to do all of that. But she acted in faith by praying to him to do something, and when he moved on her behalf, she said "yes." This is just as much an exercise of faith as her prayer. When, if ever, have you consciously said "yes" to God? What happened as a result of that "yes"?*

30. *When have you consciously said "no" to God? Why did you say "no"?*

31. *Where—if you're aware of it right now—is God calling you to act? To what do you think he wants you to say "yes"? If you're not sure, make that a topic of prayer.*

The God who made a way for my parents when I was four is the same God who is available to you now. He is the One who made a way for a Midwestern mother addicted to crack, living a life that she would not have chosen in her wildest dreams. And he is the God who we personally have seen make a way over and over again in our own lives. He watches over all of the earth, with an ear attuned to all who desire him. As the psalmist said, "The LORD is near to all who call on him, to all who call on him in truth. He fulfills the desires of those who fear him; he hears their cry and saves them" (Psalm 145:18–19).

✦ *Maybe you haven't yet said the most important "yes" to God, and that is a "yes" to his Son, Jesus. Jesus is ready to make a way for you, whatever situations or hurts you're dealing with. In fact, he has already provided a way through a problem you may not even know you have—the problem of sin. Each one of us falls far short of God's standards for our thoughts, our words, and our actions. Our sin separates us from God, but he sent Jesus to bear the punishment for our sin and to die in our place. The death of Jesus pays the penalty for our sin so that we can be in relationship with God. Accept the way that God has provided for you by praying a prayer like this:*

GOD, I NEED YOU. I AM NOT THE PERSON YOU WANT ME TO BE, AND I'M NOT DOING A VERY GOOD JOB WITH MY LIFE. PLEASE FORGIVE ME FOR FAILING TO LIVE UP TO YOUR STANDARDS AND FOR ACTING AS IF I'M THE BOSS OF MY LIFE. THANK YOU FOR SENDING JESUS TO TAKE THE PUNISHMENT FOR MY SIN AND TO DIE IN MY PLACE SO THAT YOU CAN FORGIVE ME. THANK YOU FOR MAKING THE WAY FOR ME TO BE IN RELATIONSHIP WITH YOU. TEACH ME TO LIVE WITH JESUS AS THE LEADER OF MY LIFE. AMEN.

We don't believe that you are reading this book by coincidence, any more than Marian tuned into our radio program that day by coincidence.

32. *Just why did you open up this book?*

33. *What do you hope to learn from it?*

34. *What was your initial response to the fact that you are not reading this book by coincidence?*

Just as Marian's faith made her well as she followed God's directions, we believe that you will have the same experience when you exercise your faith in God by following the eight principles we outline here. Just as you would exercise faith in a doctor by following his advice to get well physically, by following God's instructions you can get well emotionally and spiritually. God is looking for you. So join us for an exciting journey as we see the many means by which God will make a way in your life.

GOD, IT'S NOT BY ACCIDENT THAT I'VE PICKED UP THIS BOOK RIGHT NOW. YOU PLANNED FOR ME TO DO THIS. NOW PLEASE SHOW ME WHAT YOU HAVE FOR ME. SHOW ME THE PATH I NEED TO TAKE TO BE EMOTIONALLY AND SPIRITUALLY HEALTHY. THANK YOU FOR SEEKING ME OUT. IN JESUS' NAME, AMEN.

FURTHER THOUGHTS

FURTHER THOUGHTS

PRINCIPLE ONE:
BEGIN YOUR JOURNEY WITH GOD

I (Henry) was sitting on an airplane, feeling especially grateful that I had a few hours to sit back and do nothing. I was wiped out, so I was hoping for a seating companion who did not want to talk. But on this particular day, it did not happen.

When the man next to me asked, "What do you do?" I gave him the answer that's a big conversation-stopper for a lot of people: "I write books about God."

He was genuinely excited. "Oh, I'm not into God. But I do place great value in belief. I think belief is a really good thing. I've noticed that when people believe in something—in God or anything else—it seems to help them. Sort of settles them down. Gives them a sense of purpose or something like that. I don't think it really matters what they believe in. Just the fact that they believe in something is what helps."

1. *Do you think that what a person believes in matters? Explain your answer.*

2. *What beliefs are foundational for your life? Be specific. You might also note why each belief matters and how it affects the way you live.*

You may recall the story of Abraham from the Bible. We're told that he had no idea where he was headed, but he believed that God knew. He didn't just believe in belief and head out across a desert, leaving all that was familiar to go to some distant land of "promise" in some attempt to "keep the faith." No, it was much more personal than that. Abraham believed, or trusted, in a God who knew exactly where he was taking him and who was more than able to lead. Abraham knew who he was following, and he "was looking forward to the city with foundations, whose architect and builder is God" (Hebrews 11:10).

3. *Why does who we believe make a difference?*

4. *Think about the God who can make a way for you. What about his character encourages you to trust him? If you'd like to know him better, what will you do toward that end? Will you read the Bible, attend a Bible study, pray, worship, or something else? Be specific—and, if you're serious about knowing God better, ask someone to help you with this process.*

When we talk about faith, trust, and belief to carry you through, we mean it in a very specific way. Faith, trust, and belief are not just exercises of positive thinking. They involve a relationship with a very real person who knows the way for us to live and who promises to lead us in it.

By Design *(19)*

In life we all, in some situations, come to the end of our own abilities, strength, knowledge, and experience. And at that moment, just having faith in faith, or belief in belief, or even faith in ourselves is not enough. We need more.

5. *What current situation is reminding you of your limited abilities?*

We need someone greater than ourselves to tell us what to do when we don't know what to do—and that need is not a weakness. Some say that our need for God is a "crutch" and that only weak people need God. But that's not true any more than our need for air or food is because we're weak. We are *created* and *designed* to reach outside of ourselves to find the things that we need each and every day. Life is designed in a way that tells us we are not *supposed* to be able to make our own way. So I say that it does matter what you believe. More specifically, it matters whom you believe *in*. Don't believe in faith—instead, use your faith to believe in God. When we put our faith and trust in God, we've done the one thing that a human can do to accomplish superhuman things.

6. *What good news did you find in this paragraph?*

7. *If you have already put your trust in God, give an example of a time when he enabled you to accomplish superhuman things—and let this time of reflection encourage you about his ability to make a way for you in your current situation.*

8. *What skepticism, if any, did the preceding paragraph generate? What will you do to put its assertions to the test?*

We begin to find our way when we realize that we are not God. We are not limitless. We do not have all the answers because we did not make ourselves or life itself.

9. *In what area(s) of your life are you trying to be God?*

10. *As you look back over your life, when have you seen the futility of your effort to "be God"?*

God wants to show each one of us how to live the life that he's given us. Psalm 100:3 reads, "It is [God] who has made us, and not we ourselves. We are His people, and the sheep of His pasture." God is your Shepherd. Life is his pasture, and he will guide you through it. He will show you the way. Indeed, *he will actually make a way, wherever you find yourself.*

11. *Read Psalm 23. What do you most need from this Good Shepherd right now?*

12. *What, if anything, is keeping you from asking God for what you need? What will you do to overcome those barriers?*

Begin your journey with the first step of realizing that since you are not God, you are naturally going to run into the limits of your finite abilities to solve your problems or to create the life you desire. And since he is God, and he wants to be your Shepherd, you have the opportunity to live life in a relationship with the One who designed you and your life, and therefore he knows best how you can live it. That is the first step to finding out how God can make a way for you.

WHAT WE NEED . . . AND WHAT HE PROVIDES *(20)*

13. *Here's an important question to answer: What do you do when you don't know what to do?*

The sad truth is that many people do one of two things. First, we do the same thing again. We just try harder to make a relationship work, or to succeed in our careers, or to break a harmful or useless habit. This approach reflects a popular definition of insanity: *Doing the same thing over and over again but expecting different results.* The second thing most of us do at some point, when we've tried and tried with the same results, is we stop trying altogether. Understandably, we get tired and give up. So the result of trying to do life within our own limitations of strength, knowledge, and resources is futility and hopelessness.

14. *Which of these two options do you tend to take when you don't know what to do: try again or give up? Share an example or two from your own life.*

15. *Again, the result of trying to do life within our own limitations of strength, knowledge, and resources is futility and hopelessness. What current life circumstances may be pushing you toward futility and/or hopelessness?*

Fortunately, in God's economy, getting to the end of ourselves is the beginning of hope. Jesus said, "Blessed are the poor in spirit" (Matthew 5:3)—meaning that when we realize we have no more resources, we're ready to ask God for help. And the very great news is that when we ask God for help, we have instantly transcended our own limitations.

16. *If you have asked God for help regarding the circumstances you just mentioned, which of these resources have you sensed becoming available to you (see next page)? Be specific about your experience.*

Strength and power

Knowledge and wisdom

Opportunities and resources

Guidance and direction

Healing and comfort

Forgiveness and acceptance

Skill and ability

Love and community

Hope and courage

Values and principles

17. *If you haven't asked God for help regarding your circumstances, what is keeping you from doing so? Which of the resources just listed would be especially helpful?*

Here is the very heart of what we're saying in many different ways throughout this guide: *No matter what limitation or circumstances you find yourself up against in life, there is a God who can empower you and gift you to go past what you thought was possible.* It may be to help you through a hard time, deal with a difficult relationship, or even to make a dream come true. Know that God can be trusted to provide more of what you need than you ever thought possible.

18. *When, if ever, have you experienced God's empowerment in a difficult situation?*

19. *Was what God provided more of what you needed than you ever thought possible? Explain.*

20. *What kind of empowerment and support would you like to have right now? What hope does this discussion give you?*

When you're at the end of yourself, that's when Jesus can do his best work. If you have a need, there is good news! You can have God on your side.

How He Provides (23)

God's power and resources are not for special people. In fact, they cannot be earned by any human effort, ability, or goodness. They can only be received as a free gift. They can only be accessed through *humility*—that is, by realizing that we are just humans in need of our Creator.

How does God give to us today? The same way he always has: by coming to us and asking us to come to him (Revelation 3:20; John 10:10). He seeks us each and every day. All we have to do is say "yes."

21. *In what ways is God coming to you these days? Through whom or what is he asking you to come to him? Be specific.*

22. *Why is this simple "yes" to God's invitation anything but easy to do?*

The first step of how God will make a way in your life is to say "yes" to his invitation to give you all the things that you cannot provide for yourself. Instead of seeking those things, he tells us to seek him. As we do that, he will provide the "way" that we need (Matthew 6:33).

23. *Explain your understanding of seeking God rather than seeking just the blessings he can provide.*

As you read this book you'll find specific steps in the path you need to take. But without the first step—without saying "yes" to God—the principles we offer you here will just be another set of rules or concepts that you try to live out in your own strength, subject to your own limitations. To make them work, you first have to be connected to Someone larger than yourself. You have to be connected to more than mere "belief." You have to be connected to God. And when we connect to God and follow his ways, a whole new world can open up.

God, you know the ways I'm not saying "yes" to you, and you know why I'm not. Help me say "yes" to you. Show me what I need to do to strengthen my connection with you—and then help me to do it. This book just said that when I connect to you and follow your ways, a whole new world can open up. I'm ready for that, God! In Jesus' name, amen.

TAKING STEPS ALONG THE WAY:
YOUR JOURNEY WITH GOD

✦ *Where are you on your journey?* Evaluate your relationship with the Lord, its strengths and joys, its areas of weakness and struggle.

✦ *Where do you want to be?* Describe the kind of relationship with God that you desire to have.

✦ *What will you do to get there?* List two or three steps you might take toward the kind of relationship with God that you want. Choose one step to take this week—and find someone to be a helper to you for taking that step.

FURTHER THOUGHTS

FURTHER THOUGHTS

2

PRINCIPLE TWO:

CHOOSE YOUR
TRAVELING COMPANIONS WISELY

I (Henry) ran into my friend Joe, who was in the process of building a new business. He'd been working hard at putting all the pieces together, and he decided to get some input from a world-class businessman. He was hoping for some savvy "how-tos" that would make it all happen. The older man, however, responded, "I will tell you how I began my business—and it's my advice to you as well. I put together a small support group that met every week. We prayed together, confessed our struggles and sins to each other, reviewed our plans, but most of all, just supported each other. That's how I built my company."

But Joe wanted coaching about the initial funding and how to approach the banks. The successful businessman replied, "Those things are not the most important, not at the beginning. Getting your support team in place is important. Surrounding yourself with spiritually tuned, well-grounded people is the single most important first step."

1. *What is your reaction to this advice?*

Joe was hopping mad about how this guy had wasted his time offering such "useless" advice. Joe wanted to build something, make money, and accomplish his goals. What did surrounding yourself with spiritually wise people have to do with financing and sales?

Within two years Joe was broke. Not only that, he was also broken. He had decided that the man's advice would just take valuable time away from "working his plan." He could not see that getting grounded with good people should have been the first and most important part of his strategy.

2. *When, if ever, have you failed at some venture in life because you didn't surround yourself with spiritually wise people?*

3. *What current venture—business or otherwise—are you undertaking on your own? What might be the advantages of having a spiritually strong support team?*

Joe's story illustrates one of two big reasons that people do not find God's way for them. They believe that solving the problem they're facing is the most important priority, thinking that the task itself—such as getting a career going, overcoming an addiction or bad habit, or solving a difficult relationship—is the most important thing. But it's a proven fact that the work of solving a problem is secondary to getting your team together.

4. *One of the biggest reasons people fail is trying to go it alone, trying to do a better job at life without the kind of support they need from others. What areas of your life are going well right now? What kind of support do you have from other people in those areas?*

5. *If you don't have this kind of support, think of somewhere you can turn to find it.*

The other reason that some folks do not find the way that God is making for them is not the absence of good people on their team, but the *presence of not-so-good ones.* Not only do they lack people who will get them closer to their goals, but they have people who are *getting them further away* from their goals. The reality is that *some friends and acquaintances are not able to do the things that our community is supposed to do for us.* If these folks like to have fun all the time and avoid facing the growth issues in their own lives, you can bet they're unable to help you with yours. They're not going to help you grow, and it can get worse. You might have people who do more than just not help you move forward. You might have people who are actually taking you backward. And both these things can happen very subtly. Be careful about allowing such people into your vulnerabilities. Your dreams, growth, and heart are to be shared with those who can be on the side of light and life, not darkness and destruction.

6. *Consider the folks you hang out with from this perspective. Who in your life is not helping you grow?*

7. *Who in your life may actually be taking you backward? Why?*

So there are two "traveling companions" dangers: the absence of good supporters and the presence of those who hurt our cause. What we need to know is how to pick the best people to be on our personal team. Here are some things to look for in the kinds of support you are going to need.

CHOOSING YOUR TEAM *(29)*

Many people want what God has for them, but they fail to take advantage of the gifted, loving, and wise people he puts in their path. Part of God's program to make a way for you is to put good people around you who are gifted to help you get where you need to go. Some of these people will just show up in your life, sent by God at just the right time. Others you have to seek out on your own. Some will be professionals. Others may be neighbors or friends at church. As the Bible tells us, when we love and support each other, we are actually handing out the resources of God himself (1 Peter 4:10). Here are some of the things others can give to you, which are really God's gifts.

8. **Support.** *When we're going through change or trying to reach a goal, we are handling something, either good or bad, that's more than day-to-day life. We do not have these resources in and of ourselves, and God gives us this strength through the support of others. Again, list some of the members of your support team, thanking God for them, or spend a few minutes asking God where he would have you go to find solid, mature support for life's challenges.*

9. **Love.** *The Bible says, "Above all, love each other deeply, because love covers over a multitude of sins" (1 Peter 4:8). We all need a safety net of love. Love takes the sting out of life. Think of the people in your life. Who is on your side? Who is there for you? Again, if the list is small or nonexistent, ask the Lord to lead you to a place where you can know his love through his people.*

10. **Courage.** *What you have to do is not going to be without risk and fear. So we need people to say to us what the apostle Paul said to his friends: "So keep up your courage" (Acts 27:25). Who gives you courage by his or her mere presence in your life?*

11. **Feedback.** *We need feedback from others to correct us if we're going to get where we want to go in life. When, if ever, has "a wise man's rebuke" (Proverbs 25:12) helped you correct your path? Or is there someone you're avoiding today because you know deep inside that you're headed the wrong direction and you don't want to hear about it?*

12. **Wisdom.** *We do not possess all the knowledge and wisdom that we are going to need. God speaks these things into our lives through wise people. When, if ever, has God spoken knowledge and/or wisdom into your life through another human being? Be specific. To whom do you—or could you—go for wise advice when you need it?*

13. **Experience.** *In times of trouble or times of growth, we need the experience of others who have been there before. When have you been encouraged by someone who can understand your situation because of a similar experience? Why was that person such a blessing? Who is currently helping you walk through a tough situation because he or she has been there? Or where could you go to find such a person?*

14. **Modeling.** *We can't do what we have never seen, so God calls us "to imitate those who through faith and patience inherit what has been promised" (Hebrews 6:12). We learn best when we watch and learn from someone who*

is doing marriage, work, or personal growth the way we want to. Who has God put in your life as a role model? Next to each name note what you have learned or are learning from watching that person.

15. **Values.** *Your values are what guide you, and values develop in the context of community. Which of your values are supported by the people you hang out with? Be specific. What values have you learned from others?*

16. **Accountability.** *We need to be held accountable, to be "audited" by others, in order to know how we are doing and what areas need more focus. Who is close enough to you to offer such accountability? And what, if anything, do you need to do to be open rather than defensive with that person?*

The wisest man who ever lived knew the value of traveling companions. King Solomon wrote these words: "Two are better than one, because they have a good return for their work. If one falls down, his friend can help him up. But pity the man who falls and has no one to help him up! Also, if two lie down together, they will keep warm. But how can one keep warm alone? Though one may be overpowered, two can defend themselves. A cord of three strands is not quickly broken" (Ecclesiastes 4:9–12).

17. *Who comprises your "cord of three strands"? Who are the people who are there for you, on your side, pulling for you, and not afraid to tell you the truth? Which friends are available to comfort you when you are down, show you more about God than you already know, and confront you when you are headed for trouble? Who can you count on to teach you when you don't know what to do, lead you to help when you need it, cry with you when you lose, and then celebrate with you when you win?*

18. *What might have happened to my friend Joe had he put such a team in place around him?*

There are basically two kinds of people in the world: those who are growing personally and those who are going nowhere and stagnating. Welcome as traveling companions people who are pursuing God and his way for them, because they are constantly growing. They will keep you on the way God has for you. One thing has been proven over and over: *The people with the best team, win.* Make sure you are one of those people.

GOD, THANK YOU THAT I DON'T HAVE TO TRAVEL THROUGH LIFE ALL ALONE. THAT'S NOT YOUR PLAN. NOT EVEN JESUS WALKED ALONE. HE RELIED NOT ONLY ON YOU, BUT HE ALSO HAD HIS DISCIPLES AND FRIENDS LIKE MARY AND MARTHA. PLEASE HELP ME BUILD MY SUPPORT TEAM. IN JESUS' NAME, AMEN.

TAKING STEPS ALONG THE WAY:
YOUR TRAVELING COMPANIONS

✦ *Where are you on your journey?* Some of the people you need may already be in your life. If they are, thank them for their ministry to you. Tell them that you need them in order to make the next steps on your journey. Ask them if they will be available to you for accountability, feedback, or support.

✦ *Where do you want to be?* Think about the kinds of folks you need to build a strong support team. Identify which of the nine things others can give you (discussed above) that you don't yet have much of or enough of in your life.

✦ *What will you do to get there?* If you find there are not enough of these good and supportive people in your life now, then get active and find them. You might need to join a structured support group to provide the team that you need (see the sidebar on the next page).

WHAT TO LOOK FOR IN A SUPPORT GROUP

✦ A SAFE PLACE TO BRING YOUR STRUGGLE

✦ A LEADER WHO IS LOVING, HONEST, AND EXPERIENCED IN THE ISSUE

✦ INFORMATION AND TRUTH THAT PERTAINS TO THE ISSUE

✦ ACCOUNTABILITY TO GOD AND OTHERS

✦ REGULARITY OF SCHEDULE, SUCH AS MEETING TIMES AND DATES

✦ REQUIREMENTS FOR PEOPLE TO TAKE PERSONAL RESPONSIBILITY

✦ RISK-TAKING EXPERIENCES

✦ LOVING BUT DIRECT FEEDBACK AND CONFRONTATION

✦ SUPPORT AND ENCOURAGEMENT

✦ GOALS, TASKS, AND HOMEWORK ASSIGNMENTS

✦ A WAY TO USE FAILURE TO LEARN AND GROW, RATHER THAN FEELING DISCOURAGED
AND CONDEMNED BY IT

FURTHER THOUGHTS

FURTHER THOUGHTS

3

PRINCIPLE THREE:
PLACE HIGH VALUE ON WISDOM

Jan's husband found her in the garage, slumped on the floor with the bottle of pills in her hand. He knew she'd been depressed, but he had no idea that it was this bad. Nor did anyone else in her life. Jan was a very accomplished woman who had a lot of friends. No one would have guessed she was suicidal unless she had told them, and she was not about to tell anyone.

Jan's husband took her to the hospital where I (Henry) interviewed her. "I have no hope at all," she told me with a blank stare. "None. And I know nothing will ever change for me. I'm just stuck down here in this depression. And no one gets it."

Sure that she would never feel better, she protested being in the hospital. "I can't let you go home," I said. "But I do believe you will get better. I know that you can't see that right now. From your perspective at the moment, there is no way out. But from my perspective, given what I know, there is a way. You just can't see it yet."

1. *How does having the big picture help us see our problems in a different way?*

2. *What current situation in your life or circumstances that seems impossible to you might look different from someone else's perspective?*

Wisdom Makes the Difference *(37)*

Years of clinical experience have taught me something very valuable about life and how God makes a way. While many people who check into the hospital or come to see me for counseling feel there is no hope, I can feel *with total certainty* that what they are experiencing will be resolved. One person is certain that it's all over. Another is certain that the victory is guaranteed. What's the difference? In one word: wisdom.

3. *What is wisdom? Share your own ideas, describe a wise person you know, and/or open a dictionary.*

Wisdom is skill and knowledge applied to living, and I have learned some principles of wisdom—true and tested principles of God's ways—by which people can resolve seemingly insoluble problems. For instance, if depression was something that I had seen resolved before, and there were tested treatments that I knew worked, I had hope from the *wisdom* that good teachers had passed on to me. I knew that the depressed person would get well.

My point is actually the same one that God makes in the Book of Proverbs, when he says that hope comes from wisdom: "Know also that wisdom is sweet to your soul; *if you find it, there is a future hope for you,* and your hope will not be cut off" (Proverbs 24:14; emphasis ours).

4. *When have you known something (wisdom) that enabled you to give another person hope? Be specific. (If you're a parent, you might talk about a situation involving a child.)*

5. *When has someone else's wisdom given you hope? Again, be specific.*

Many times we feel hopeless because we do not know what to do next. When we add to that the sense that maybe nothing can be done, things do indeed seem hopeless. But the reality is that God has no limit when it comes to solutions. He can and will make a way. Sometimes, as he tells us, the path to that way is *helping us to gain wisdom as it applies to our situation.*

6. *Look up the following scriptures to see how much God values wisdom:*
    Proverbs 2:12
    Proverbs 4:7
    Proverbs 19:8

Over and over the Bible tells us that one path God uses to make a way is to give us wisdom. Our task is to find out what we do not know about what we are going through and what will help. So here are a few things to remember about the process of gaining wisdom.

WISDOM AND TRUTH COME FROM GOD *(39)*

The first place we need to look for wisdom is directly from God himself.

7. *Write out the promise of James 1:5.*

8. *What sort of wisdom do you need right now? Ask God for it!*

GOD USES THE WISDOM OF OTHERS *(40)*

There are many situations you and I do not know how to handle. But the reality is, someone knows how to resolve our problem. Our job is to find that someone.

9. *Why is prayer a good first step toward finding that someone?*

10. *After we pray, we need to actively seek those who have experience in whatever we're struggling with. Among the people already in your life, whom can you go to for help in the following areas?*

   Finances

   Job/career decisions

   Spiritual guidance

   Marriage

   Parenting

   Other

11. *Where can you go to find someone who might be a resource for you? When will you do so?*

SEEK STRUCTURED WISDOM *(40)*

The areas in which we struggle have usually been addressed, and there is some sort of formal help available if we look. (By "formal," I mean someone who is skilled in the form of help we need.) There are grief programs, divorce recovery programs, couples groups, financial debt relief counselors, résumé writing courses, job interview coaches . . . and on and on. There is no need for you to reinvent the wheel. It's sad to see people staying stuck and not seeking wisdom and help—when it's so widely available! And today cost does not have to be an obstacle because many fine programs are available through churches and government agencies.

12. *What keeps people in general from seeking wisdom and help?*

13. *What is keeping you from seeking wisdom and help?*

A woman I talked with at a seminar wanted to go back to school and become a musician, but "God is not providing the money," she said. I asked her, "How many granting agencies have you applied to? How many scholarships have you sought? How many people who have heard you sing and minister with this gift have you asked to support you in reaching this dream?" She blinked.

This woman had just assumed that the money was not there. And she assumed, because she had prayed a few times and cash did not show up miraculously, that God was not providing. I told her, "Go and seek help from people who know how to get grants. Apply to a zillion places. If you've done that and still get no help, then you can say God has not provided and the door to that dream is closed. But not until then."

14. *What does this woman's experience suggest, if anything, about a dream of yours that is not yet realized or a prayer not yet answered?*

15. *What do you do to regularly gain more knowledge and wisdom? Consider these sources:*

Pastors

Church programs

Community colleges

Seminars

Books and tapes

Workshops

Retreats

Professionals

Self-help groups

TEST THE VOICES OF WISDOM *(43)*

The Bible says we should make it a goal to get wisdom, even though the cost might be high (Proverbs 4:7). But you can waste your money buying "wisdom" and experiences that are worthless. As we seek wisdom, it's important to be sure the people who offer wise counsel know what they're talking about.

16. *Why is it important to "test the voices of wisdom"?*

17. *If you are currently relying on a formal source of wisdom, what did you do— or will you do—to test that person's voice?*

Do not believe every so-called expert or put your trust in quick-answer "solutions." Check the track record. Get a good referral from someone who is familiar with a counselor's work. Remember, just because someone says that he or she is an expert does not make it so.

NOT A RANDOM UNIVERSE *(43)*

God has put you in a universe that has order. There are principles that govern relationships, work, the way you feel, and the like. Things work or don't work because of laws that have been in place since God first created everything. The Bible says, "By wisdom the LORD laid the earth's foundations, by understanding he set the heavens in place; by his knowledge the deeps were divided, and the clouds let drop the dew" (Proverbs 3:19–20).

18. *Why is it important to realize that the universe has order?*

19. *What bearing does this order have on your own personal spiritual growth?*

Part of the way God has laid out for you through your dilemma has probably already been made. Your job is to find that way by seeking the wisdom that applies to your troubled situation. One thing is sure: We can depend on God's ways to work. So ask him for help, seek wisdom with all your strength, and then when you find it, apply it with all that you are.

GOD, I'M GLAD YOU'LL GIVE ME WISDOM WHEN I ASK YOU FOR IT. PLEASE ALSO GUIDE ME TO PEOPLE WHO CAN BE SOURCES OF THE WISDOM I NEED. THANK YOU FOR THE WISE PEOPLE WHO ARE ALREADY IN MY LIFE. AND, LORD, WHEN I HEAR YOUR WISDOM, MAY I RECOGNIZE IT AS SUCH AND THEN DO WHAT YOU WANT ME TO DO. IN JESUS' NAME, AMEN.

Taking Steps Along the Way:
Valuing and Seeking Wisdom

✦ *Where are you on your journey?* Identify sources of wisdom already in your life.

✦ *Where do you want to be?* None of us is an expert in everything. List areas of your life where you would benefit from greater knowledge and wisdom.

✦ *What will you do to get there?* Consider possible sources of the knowledge and wisdom you need. Don't rule out people you are already in relationship with or more formal sources of wisdom. And don't forget to pray for God's guidance and the gift of insight he can give.

FURTHER THOUGHTS

FURTHER THOUGHTS

4

Principle Four:
Leave Your Baggage Behind

G len was excited about his new job with the marketing department of a family-owned company that sold medical supplies. He was hired to build relationships with doctors, hospital administrators, and other key influencers in the medical community that the sales force could follow up on. To an outgoing guy like Glen, having a job that primarily involved building relationships with people was a dream come true.

Things were going well—until about the third week when accounting called to remind him that he hadn't turned in his receipts or expense report. A few days later Glen's boss, John, called: The CFO had contacted him about that paperwork that had never been turned in. Later that week, Glen failed to submit an important research report to top management for the annual meeting of the board of directors. When John tried to address these issues with Glen, he reacted with anger and sarcasm.

Eventually, Glen's talents and contributions could not outweigh his poor administrative performance. Regretfully to all the managers who had had such great hopes for him, he was let go. Yet Glen's problems would continue to plague his wife and daughters through two more jobs and job losses. His family had to move and start over twice, until Glen finally figured it out—and God made a way for him to move past his past.

1. *What, if anything, does Glen's story help you see about patterns in your own life?*

2. *What hope do you find in this account of Glen's time with the company?*

CHECK IN YOUR BAGGAGE *(48)*

We all have relationships, experiences, and lessons in life that are sometimes painful, difficult, and, for whatever reason, hard to process. As a result, we walk around with certain feelings, patterns, and conflicts that do not really relate to the present but to people and events from a previous time. Because those things are not "finished," they get in the way of present situations, present relationships, or present goals. And the sad thing is, this "baggage" that we carry around does not go away until it is dealt with, or "finished."

3. *What relationships, experiences, and lessons in your life have been painful and hard to process?*

4. *In what ways and situations have you noticed these events from the past affecting you in the present? Be specific.*

Glen's "baggage" was his relationship with his father. Glen's dad had been a strong, overbearing man. Glen felt he could never please him. He always felt put down and unappreciated. As a result, Glen was deeply hurt and developed a sensitivity to criticism, for good reason.

In many ways, his dad was just mean. So Glen felt "one-down" in comparison to others. As he grew older, Glen worked hard to overcome those feelings. He performed well and tried hard. But with any criticism, even *constructive criticism,* he would go into a time warp and begin to feel just as he'd felt as a kid. Sadly, he'd act like a child and then lose his job, and his wife and daughters would suffer. His patterns of resisting authority, being indirect, and not fulfilling his boss's expectations would catch up with him.

5. *What insight into yourself, your patterns, and your own life did you gain from this discussion of Glen's patterns and their source?*

6. *If hurtful things have happened to you and you have not yet dealt with them, those old events will continue to produce what we refer to as "issues" in your life.* In a very real sense, your past will become your present. *To see where*

this is happening, describe any "time warp" moments when you, like Glen, feel just as you did as a kid.

The Book of Proverbs reveals, "Keep thy heart with all diligence; for out of it are the issues of life" (Proverbs 4:23, KJV). Glen had hurts in his heart that were affecting him. When he received correction from a boss in the present, he felt as if he were dealing with his unreasonable father. He needed to "keep his heart," so that he could be free from the past and have a new present.

Rescue Your Heart from the Past *(50)*

So how does God make a way for us to leave behind our old baggage from the past? Here are six steps you can ask God to help you take.

A. **Agree that you have a problem from the past, and confess it.** No issue can be overcome until we admit that it exists and no feeling—whether anger, or passion, or "numb"—exists for no reason.

When Karen called into our radio program about her lack of desire for sex with her husband, she didn't see any connection between the current problem and the sexual abuse she had experienced earlier in her life. Until she could acknowledge that the significant and damaging events in her past had a major effect on her now, she could not work through them. *And as long as she could not work through those experiences, they continued to be present, not past.*

7.   *What problem from your past might be affecting your present?*

God's word for "agree" is the word that is translated "confess." To confess something means that we agree that it is true. When it comes to baggage that is bothering us, we must recognize that things have gone wrong—either to us or by us—and agree with God, or "confess," that they happened and affected us deeply.

8.   *What keeps people from "confessing" those things that have gone wrong in their past? What has kept or is keeping you from doing so?*

B. **Get healing and express grief.** The next step is to receive the care and healing we need to deal with whatever has happened to wound us. If your heart has been broken, then you have to allow others to give you God's care and love to help mend that broken heart. Also, our past losses and hurts can be healed as we allow ourselves to attach to them the sadness that's warranted. Simply put, we need to grieve. Ecclesiastes 7:3 says, "Sorrow is better than laughter, because a sad face is good for the heart." If Glen and Karen could allow themselves to face their grief, then his sensitive heart to criticism, and her frightened heart from abuse, could begin to heal. They could take in the love that God and others would have for them, love that people from their past did not give. Then they would be able to be more in the present and less in the pain and feelings of the past. And the same is true for you and me.

9. *Glen needed some loving people to talk to about how his father had hurt him and to validate that his pain was warranted. Karen needed someone to mourn with her and to help process the fear and hurt that accompany sexual abuse so that it could lose its power. What kind of healing might you need?*

10. *For what do you need to grieve—and when will you give yourself permission and the opportunity to do so?*

C. **Receive forgiveness.** Many times the pain that we drag into new situations is the pain of failure from the past. If you are feeling guilty or ashamed of things that you have done, you cannot tackle life with gusto. Leaving our baggage behind means that we have to know we are totally accepted, forgiven, and loved. That kind of forgiveness and love is the kind of love that God has for all of us. All we have to do is ask for it and receive it.

11. *Write out the promises of the following verses:*
    Psalm 103:11–12
    1 John 1:9
    Hebrews 8:12

12. *For what have you not received the forgiveness that God has for you? Be specific as you confess your sin to him and ask for his forgiveness.*

13. *When we sin or fail, we tend to think that others will not accept us. What does James 5:16 tell us about confessing our sins to others?*

14. *One of the most powerful ways God makes a way out of our past failures is for us to talk to each other—and to pray for one another. To whom will you turn to confess your past sin and/or failure so that your failures will not continue to alienate you? And when will you meet to pray with that person? Failures will lose their grip in the light of acceptance and prayer.*

D. **Forgive others.** Resentment and lack of forgiveness tie us to the offenses that initially caused those feelings. To the degree we have not forgiven, everyone who has ever hurt us still hurts us every day. God has provided a way for us to be free of past debts that are owed—the same way that he takes care of our debts: forgiveness. When *we* forgive others, we are free.

15. *What circumstances from your past do you resent? Who have you failed to forgive?*

16. *Why haven't you forgiven the person(s) involved in the situations you just identified?*

To forgive does not mean that we deny that someone has hurt us. Nor does it mean that we have to necessarily trust them again or allow them into our heart again. That depends on whether they've seen the error of their ways and repented. But forgiveness is not about the future and whether we are going to open up and be vulnerable again. It's about letting go of what has already happened. It's about acknowledging both the things that were done to harm us and the debt that we are owed.

17. *What about this definition of forgiveness is new and/or especially helpful to you?*

18. *What benefits will you enjoy once you forgive people from your past?*

E. **Examine your ways.** We've talked about hurts—but a significant part of the baggage of the past has to do with patterns of behavior that we learned from those hurtful situations. And the list of self-defeating patterns we can develop is almost endless. The principle for all of them is the same: *Patterns we have learned in the past can be baggage ruining our present.*

As a young boy, Glen learned that authority—any authority—was unreasonable and impossible to please. So he passively avoided his father and resisted doing what was asked. He also avoided talking to his father directly about their conflicts. As a result, Glen never learned to solve problems and get past them. That's why a late expense report, which was a small oversight, could grow into something that could end his career.

19. *What pattern of dealing with life, people, relationships, risk, or even love itself is causing you problems right now?*

20. *Has life taught you that relationships are only going to hurt you and so you've learned not to let people get close? Do you avoid conflict? Are you avoiding any risk in an attempt to maintain control? If you're not sure what patterns, if any, have a hold on you, talk to someone who knows you well.*

F. **See the new you through new eyes.** Another kind of baggage we carry around is the view of ourselves that we learned in past relationships or situations. Glen learned that he was not good enough. Karen learned that she was an object for someone to use. He would be hurt, and she would be afraid. Both are very understandable, for that is how God made us. *We find out who we are through the people who love us or, sometimes, through the ones who don't.*

21. *When you were young, what did you learn about yourself—true or not true—from the people who loved you and/or from the people who didn't?*

22. *Included in the baggage we all need to unpack are the various false views of ourselves that we learned in past relationships. Do an inventory about how you see yourself. Answer these questions as specifically as possible:*
   Is the way I see myself realistic?

   Is it balanced with strengths and weakness, of things I value and areas in which I need to grow?

   Do I see myself as loved?

God has designed us to learn who we are by who loves us. We need—deeply need—to see ourselves first of all as loved by God and having great value to him. Then we can begin to see ourselves as the people who love us can see us. In this way we begin to unpack the baggage of old views that are holding us back.

BE FREE TO BE YOU *(57)*

If the Bible tells any story at all, and if believers around the world have any story to tell, it is the story of a God who frees us from enslavement to the past. He has been releasing people from the weight of painful old baggage since time began.

23. *What story of God's freeing you from past enslavement can you tell?*

24. *What story of his freeing you from past enslavement would you like to be able to tell?*

25. *What hurt, unforgiveness, or other dysfunctional ties to the past do you need to deal with so that your past does not hold you back?*

God has made a way out from under the baggage of the past, and a way to unpack your bags of grief, pain, unforgiveness, guilt, shame, or even old patterns of relating.

GOD, THANK YOU FOR ALWAYS BEING READY TO FORGIVE ME—AND THANK YOU FOR HELPING ME FORGIVE OTHERS SO THAT I DON'T HAVE TO CARRY AROUND THE BAGGAGE OF PAST HURTS. HELP ME TO GRIEVE WHAT I NEED TO GRIEVE, TO CONFESS WHAT I NEED TO CONFESS TO YOU AND TO OTHERS, TO FORGIVE THOSE I NEED TO FORGIVE, AND TO ACCEPT A HEALTHIER VIEW OF MYSELF BASED IN YOUR AMAZING LOVE FOR ME. THANK YOU THAT YOU CAN HELP ME BE FREE OF THE PAIN OF MY PAST. IN JESUS' NAME, AMEN.

TAKING STEPS ALONG THE WAY:
LEAVING THE PAST BEHIND

✦ *Where are you on your journey?* List any painful old baggage from the past you are still carrying. Include any kind of grief, pain, unforgiveness, guilt, shame, patterns of relating, and/or view of yourself that you are lugging around.

✦ *Where do you want to be?* Next to each item you listed, write out what you want to do about it. Describe the healthier position you would like to be in.

✦ *What will you do to get there?* Ask God to show you his ways of unpacking your heavy baggage so you can begin to travel light—and choose one item to work on this week as well as someone who will walk the path with you. If you follow God's guidance, you'll begin to experience more happiness, better relationships, and more fulfillment than you ever thought possible.

FURTHER THOUGHTS

FURTHER THOUGHTS

5

PRINCIPLE FIVE:

OWN YOUR FAULTS AND WEAKNESSES

Sharon—I am leaving. I'll call you with my new number. We'll need to discuss the kids and finances. I'm sorry things aren't working out. Rob.

Numbly, Sharon looked around the kitchen. She felt surreal and disoriented. Waves of hurt, fear, and sadness overwhelmed her. She was aware that she and Rob had not been doing well and that he was miserable in the marriage. She was also aware of the stress they'd been through recently with a relocation due to Rob's job. She attributed most of their struggle to the move. But the fact was, long before the move there were serious seeds of discontent in their marriage.

You see, Sharon had a certain spiritual blindness that she had never allowed God to touch, help, or heal. *She was one of those people who has great difficulty taking responsibility for their life.* In Sharon's mind, whenever a problem arose, it was always the fault of someone other than her. She would blame others, excuse herself, and not admit to her part in the problem. Most of the time, the blame went to Rob, since he was the person closest to her. There was not enough love, time, or support to make her happy. Whatever was wrong was always entirely his fault.

1. *What about yourself, if anything, do you see in this description of Sharon?*

2. *What factors keep people from accepting responsibility for their life?*

SOMETIMES IT TAKES A SHOCK *(62)*

Sometimes we need a shock to wake us up to the truth.

3. *When have you been shocked into realizing the truth about a situation? Be specific.*

4. *Why do we sometimes need to be shocked to face a truth? Again, be specific.*

Sharon had refused for months to consider that her constant blaming was at the root of their marriage problems. She could not see that her behavior hurt Rob so much that it made him doubt that he was loved by God or anyone. Fortunately, Sharon loved God, and she reached out to him by praying and asking him to help. Nothing happened—at least not right then. Reality didn't shift. There were no signs, signals, or voices to heed. But Sharon didn't give up on God. He was her only hope, so she kept praying.

Often God allows us to wrestle for long periods of time as we reach out for him. At one of the most painful times of his life, Jesus prayed three times without any noticeable response from God (Matthew 26:39–44). It is as if God is helping us to truly own our pleas, wishes, and desires.

5. *When has God allowed you to wrestle with him in prayer and to wait on him to act in response to your prayers? What benefit(s) resulted from that wrestling and waiting?*

6. *What current issue or situation in your life has long been a topic of prayer and discussion with God?*

7. *What comfort do you find in the fact that God allowed Jesus to wrestle with him in prayer and apparently receive no noticeable response?*

8. *What current issue or situation in your life could be a topic of prayer, discussion, or even wrestling with God?*

Sharon continued to pray, to search, and to listen for an answer. Within a few days, something began to happen in her heart. She began to feel something inside—emotions that had to do with Rob. As she explained it later, she began to feel *his* hurt. She stopped feeling the pain he'd caused her and instead felt the pain that *she'd* caused *him*. With this clearer perspective, Sharon could not believe how hurtful she'd been. She deeply felt the rejection and injury that she had caused Rob. Along with that, she felt great remorse and anguish for his hurt. The jolt she'd gotten from Rob, coupled with God's grace in showing her the truth about her actions, had done their work.

9. *What encouragement do you find at this point of Rob and Sharon's story?*

10. *What hope does it give you for a challenge you are currently facing? What idea for a course of action?*

THE TRUTH CAN STING—BUT IT SETS YOU FREE *(64)*

This process in which God gently opened up Sharon's heart went on for some days. It was not pleasant. She was constantly facing her lack of ownership for her own failures and the neglecting of her responsibility toward Rob. She didn't like herself very much during this period of God-given clarity. Still, she kept praying for God's help and strength to bear the truth. And she desperately wanted his solutions.

At the same time, Sharon was discovering a deeper sense of appreciation and love for Rob. Now that she was shouldering her rightful share of the blame for their problems, it was as if there was more room inside her to see his good parts. She seemed to hear from God, *Go to Rob and make it right.* So she met with him and sincerely apologized for the many years of heaping blame on him and for not acknowledging her own problems and failures.

Rob was stunned. He was *sure* God must have done something to change Sharon. He began to open up his bruised and untrusting heart to her, his first love. He was immediately willing to try to connect with Sharon again, and she with him.

11. *Again, what encouragement do you find at this point of Rob and Sharon's story?*

12. *What hope does it give you for a challenge you are currently facing? What idea for a course of action?*

Sharon had realized she needed to learn how to take ownership of her own failings. With some counseling, though, she also learned that she had to take responsibility for the *patterns* of her life and change her behavior. It is one thing to say you are sorry you stepped on your dancing partner's feet; it is another to take some lessons so you don't keep doing it!

13. *Whose feet have you stepped on? Were you able to feel remorse and apologize to that person?*

14. *What lessons did you take or should you take so you don't keep stepping on that person's feet?*

When she first reached out to God in prayer, Sharon thought God would show Rob the error of his ways. She was surprised that God answered her prayer by showing her that she needed to learn to shoulder the burdens of ownership of her life. As Jesus said, "If anyone would come after me, he must deny himself and take up his cross daily and follow me" (Luke 9:23).

15. *In what area of your life is Jesus calling you to deny yourself and follow him? Be specific.*

16. *What support are you getting so that you can obey? Who is holding you accountable in your efforts?*

As Sharon's story illustrates, the greatest miracles are often those God brings about in the quiet of the human heart.

Implement the Principle of Ownership *(67)*

Ownership is a stance a person takes toward life, goals, and issues that says, *My life is my problem. Whatever I want, need, or desire, God has a part for me to play in getting it. Whatever dreams God gives me or problems I need to resolve, I can take part in furthering my goals.*

As the psalmist declared, "The LORD is my rock, my fortress and my deliverer; my God is my rock, in whom I take refuge. He is my shield and the horn of my salvation, my stronghold" (Psalm 18:2). Yet as God does his job, we are to do ours. The apostle Paul said, "Continue to work out your salvation with fear and trembling, for it is God who works in you to will and to act according to his good purpose" (Philippians 2:12–13).

"Work out your salvation" means that now that God has delivered and saved us, we are to take responsibility to live a life that reflects him and his ways: daily dependence on God, trust, love, honesty, and all the things that are of him. And while we are doing that, he is doing miraculous, divine things to achieve his ends.

17. *What new insight or greater understanding did you gain from these three paragraphs?*

18. *What is God saying to you here about a particular situation in your own life? Be specific.*

19. *In what area(s) of your life do you need to take "ownership" by reflecting God and his ways?*

Sharon was a colaborer with God. God sent friends, let Rob move out but not file for divorce, and opened Sharon's heart to her blindness about herself. Sharon searched, listened, remained open, did not give up on God, and finally became responsible to the light he was pointing her way. Like Sharon, we need to learn that God prepares a way, and we take ownership to put our feet on the path and walk it.

TAKE OWNERSHIP, FAULT, AND BLAME *(68)*

Some people struggle with the fact that they are not always the cause of their problems. A man whose company lays him off because of the economy may feel that he is owed another job because the layoff wasn't of his doing. No one would disagree that we aren't the cause of all our problems. But, in terms of solving the issue, fault is irrelevant. Here's a much more helpful way of thinking: The person who cares about the problem owns the problem.

20. *What problem(s) in your life were you not the cause of?*

21. *What current problem(s) are you not the cause of?*

22. *In each case, why is fault ultimately irrelevant—and why is it important to acknowledge that fact?*

Ownership empowers us to act—to use our various skills to make plans, tackle a hurtful situation, or right a wrong. People who "own" their problems are people who can take initiative. Ownership also gives us freedom. You are no longer a slave to the past, to false hope, to wishing someone would change, or to discouragement and passivity. Ownership is, in fact, a blessing. It feels uncomfortable at first, but it pays off later.

23. *When have you experienced the empowerment of "owning" a problem or situation? The freedom that comes with ownership? The blessing of ownership?*

24. *What kinds of payoff might you enjoy if you took ownership where you need to?*

In contrast to the blessing of ownership is the curse of blame, when we project all the responsibility for a problem onto something or someone else. There is a time when some blame can help us, but what I (John) mean by "blame" here is the process of assessing the responsibilities in a given situation. We should go through a kind of spiritual audit process to figure out who contributed what to the problem. Assessing this type of blame can instruct us about what we need to forgive. At the same time, if we did have a part in the problem, we are to confess, ask forgiveness, and repent. A period of assessment can help us ferret out the roots of a problem. Remember, though, the problem and its solution are the real issues—not who caused the problem.

25. *Why is blame—projecting all the responsibility for a problem onto someone or something else—a common course of action?*

26. *For what are you blaming someone rather than choosing to take ownership? Be honest with yourself.*

27. *Perform a spiritual audit on any current and pressing problem. What did you contribute to the situation? Who do you need to forgive? From whom do you need to ask forgiveness? When will you take these steps of forgiveness?*

28. *Explain why the real issues are the problem and its solution, not who caused the problem.*

LEARN WHAT TO OWN *(69)*

If you want God to make a way in your life, own your own faults and weaknesses. God blesses ownership. Here is a brief list of things for which you can begin to take responsibility, and in this way be a colaborer with God.

A. **Your own unhappiness.** Ask God to help you take ownership of the pain or discomfort you're feeling and then ask him to help you find relief.

B. **Specific issues.** Determine the root cause of your problem (a relationship disconnect, a faith journey, a job issue, or a habit that won't go away).

C. **Needed resources.** Get the help, support, comfort, advice, answers, and encouragement you need to solve your problem.

D. **Weaknesses and obstacles.** Identify and begin to develop the areas in which you don't have enough strength to meet the challenge.

E. **Accountability.** Submit yourself to a few people who will keep you on task resolving your struggle or meeting your goal.

F. **Support team.** Seek out compassionate friends who offer comfort but who will not let you shirk your responsibilities.

G. **One day at a time.** Address the issues of today rather than obsessing about yesterday or hoping for rescue tomorrow.

29. *Which of these items, if any, surprise you?*

30. *Which one will you tackle this week—and what will you do? Be specific.*

Finally, resist the temptation to take all the blame for everything. Your struggle is not for you to bear alone. God has his part, and he will gladly act on your behalf. Neither your shoulders nor mine are wide enough to carry it all.

31. *For what have you been taking all the blame?*

32. *What will you do to stop, to release some of the blame?*

The good news is, when we take ownership, life works better. That's because when we do things God's way, he is there helping us to carry the burden. As Jesus said, "My yoke is easy, and my burden is light" (Matthew 11:30).

33. *When have you seen life work better (your own or someone else's) because you took ownership? Describe the situation.*

34. *What current burden do you need to let Jesus help you carry?*

God, I'm not very good at owning my faults and weaknesses —and I'm not even sure I want to learn how to do that. So please first help me want to learn to take responsibility for them. Then please go easy on me as you show me the truth about myself. But I may need a shock. If that's the case, help me be aware that you're with me as I deal with the emotions and ideas that come with the truth about who I am. In Jesus' name, amen.

Taking Steps Along the Way:
Owning Your Faults and Weaknesses

✦ *Where are you on your journey?* Note the last opportunity you had to take healthy and complete ownership of your fault, your sin, or your weakness. Point out what, if anything, you would do to handle the situation better if you had a second chance.

✦ *Where do you want to be?* Describe what owning your faults and weaknesses would look like (in your marriage, your dating relationships, the working world, etc.).

✦ *What will you do to get there?* Commit to regular prayer about your lack of ownership of your faults and weaknesses. If possible, talk to someone who gracefully takes responsibility for his or her own faults and weaknesses. Learn from that role model.

FURTHER THOUGHTS

FURTHER THOUGHTS

6

PRINCIPLE SIX:
EMBRACE PROBLEMS AS GIFTS

When I (John) met my friend Gary for breakfast, he abruptly announced, "I've been fired." Fired? I was shocked. Gary was a seasoned, upper-level management professional in a large manufacturing firm. But personnel restructuring at the upper levels had left him with a new boss, and Gary and Dan did not hit it off well. Gary tried to fit into Dan's system, but he was unable to meet his boss's goals and expectations. After protracted and painful attempts to remedy the issue, Gary was let go.

When I asked Gary what I could do, his answer surprised me: "John, I want you to pray that I will learn whatever it is God wants me to learn in this situation. I have no idea what's next, but I know God is behind all of this. So I figure the best way to deal with my crisis is to begin with God. Learning what God wants me to learn seems like the best approach."

1. *What do you appreciate about Gary's approach to his job loss?*

2. *To what current problem can you apply Gary's approach? From what situation could you be learning a lesson that God wants you to learn?*

For the next few months, Gary didn't wallow in self-pity or blaming. Rather, every day he questioned and investigated God's way for him. At the same time he conducted an energetic and relentless job search that landed him a good position with another firm. He's still there today and doing fine.

Had Gary concentrated all his energies on the job search, no one would have blamed him. He had a family to take care of and bills to pay. That would have been a good thing to do. *But it would not have been the best thing.* The "best thing" was that Gary asked God to teach him something. Gary's faith directed him to search for whatever lesson, change, or growth was behind his loss. He knew that the best thing is to see problems as windows to the face of God and to stand at that window until God shows us the light that illuminates our hearts. Gary wanted to walk through his dilemma God's way. That was because Gary's faith told him that he could trust God to take care of him.

3. *Describe a problem, fully resolved or not, that has proven to be a window to the face of God. What did you learn—about God, about yourself—from that particular dilemma?*

4. *Why is the ability to trust God key to embracing problems as gifts?*

Gary learned a lot about himself as he searched, asked, prayed, read the Bible, and talked to people. Once he gained that understanding, he went to work changing and growing. Now he seems more alive inside. He tries new things, he's more open to experience, and he mentors men who need career assistance. Gary used his problem to find God in a new and better way.

A MATTER OF PERSPECTIVE *(73)*

Like Gary, we all have problems. They are part of life. But how we solve our problems divides us into two groups: *those who end at the problem and those who go beyond the problem.* The first group of people has a tendency to stop dead in their tracks when they hit a crisis, and that's where they stay. The second group, like Gary, finds something useful in problems.

 5. *Which approach to problems do you tend to take? Give evidence from your life.*

There's nothing wrong with trying to solve the problem and alleviate the pain. But the way *out* of our problems shouldn't be our first concern, because God sees our difficulties very differently than we do. In a very real sense, they are his gifts to us, for they bring us to him and his ways. He has many, many lessons and a new life for us as we learn to go *through* problems—and God is not as concerned with getting us out of problems as he is in getting us through problems.

 6. *What does that last sentence mean to you?*

7. *When has a problem actually seemed like something of a gift to you?*

8. *Which current problem or challenge you're facing just might be a gift from God?*

When you go to the doctor in pain, you can demand immediate relief, knowing that your physical problem will recur, or you can go through the healing process (surgery, physical therapy) and resolve the problem once and for all. That's the same kind of choice you face when dealing with life's problems and crises. God loves you completely and wants the best for you. But like your physician, *he is less concerned about your immediate comfort than about your long-term health and growth.*

9. *If you are a parent, describe a time when you acted out of concern for your child's long-term health and growth rather than his or her immediate comfort.*

10. *What does this parent-child analogy and the paragraph that precedes it reveal to you about a problem you have experienced or are now experiencing?*

Instead of looking for a way out of your problems, you may want to consider two other places to look that will get you through them: *upward* and *inward.*

The Two Directions *(75)*

First, we can allow our problems to turn us *upward*. We can shift our focus off the issue itself and onto how God sees it. Problems give us an opportunity to look beyond our small world, our familiar answers and trusted habits, and peer out into the unknown, where God is waiting. When we look upward, we open up to God—and God also opens himself up to us.

11. *What do you think God's perspective is on one or two of the challenges you currently face?*

12. *What benefits come with God's opening himself up to us?*

Besides looking upward, we look *inward*. Once the problem drives us upward to God, he then takes us on a journey into ourselves to demonstrate what he wants us to learn. He helps us understand what is going on inside us—that is, in terms of our attitudes and reactions. He lights up hurts, wounds, weaknesses, and opinions that need *his* touch and *our* submission to him. Singles, for instance, can ask God to help them look inward and learn what happened in the train wrecks of past breakups. They see what contributed to each relationship's problems or if they allowed themselves to be drawn to the wrong person. They ask God what they need to change in order to pick the right person. Allowing God to open our eyes and give us the inward view of ourselves bears a lot of good fruit.

13. *What good fruit have you enjoyed—what lessons about yourself have you learned—because you took the inward view of a problem?*

14. *What current problem will you risk asking God to give you an inward view of?*

When we look inward, God reveals that we have certain central issues that are like attitudinal foundation stones. They form reactions that occur in not just one but in many areas of life. Gary, whom we met at the beginning of the chapter, found that he was fearful of risks and anything new. Besides affecting his work, Gary realized, his fear of taking risks impacted his relationships as well. While he cared and was kind to his family, he avoided the risk of being vulnerable and exposing how he felt about things.

15. *Identify issues that are your "attitudinal foundation stones."*

16. *When has one of those stones affected more than one aspect of your life? Give details.*

God does help us identify themes, or patterns, in our lives. And as we patiently let God do so, we are able to see how these patterns affect much more of our life than we ever imagined.

17. *This week ask God to help you identify the themes in your life. When he does, then ask him to help you learn from those patterns and grow.*

SEEING PAIN AS NORMAL *(77)*

Problems are also a gift in that they help us *normalize* pain—that is, they help us expect pain to be a regular part of life. We do not like to experience problems or pain as part of life. We wish life to be different than it is. So when pain and struggle occur, we protest, deny, or argue that these things should not be. But life is difficult, and all our resistance does nothing to alter the reality of pain.

18. *What tends to be your response to pain and struggle?*

When we give up protesting about pain and problems, we begin letting go of things that we can't keep anyway, things we can't change and therefore must adapt to (things like a lost relationship that is gone for good or a work opportunity that we didn't go for and now the window is closed). We also accept that pain is part of life. We accept that we don't have all the answers. We accept that problems will always be around us. We accept that there are some problems that will remain mysteries until we are face to face with God. That acceptance helps us to live in God's reality, which in turn allows us to adapt and change to the way things really are. It also allows us to relax and become flexible, so that God can more easily direct us through our problems.

19. *Which problems in your life have you accepted as remaining mysteries until you are face to face with God?*

20. *Why is it helpful to see pain as normal? What advantages come with accepting problems as part of life?*

IDENTIFYING WITH SUFFERING *(78)*

Problems are a gift in yet another way: They help us identify with the sufferings of God. He has chosen the path of suffering for himself. He deals with problems even when they hurt him. He faces the problem (ever since Adam and Eve we human beings have been a problem for God) and takes responsibility for doing something about it. And while he is redeeming, restoring, forgiving, repairing, and healing us, he suffers from what we put him through.

21. *What have the problems in your life taught you about God?*

22. *What have those problems helped you understand about Jesus' journey to the cross?*

We can learn much from our problems as we allow ourselves to come closer to God's suffering, especially through Jesus, "the author and perfecter of our faith, who for the joy set before him endured the cross" (Hebrews 12:2). When we identify with God's sufferings, we are deepened and matured. So don't ask God to get rid of problems. He knows that is not best for you. Much of life is moving from problem to problem. See problems as the next steps of growth for you, embrace them, and move along—looking upward and inward—with him.

23. *What maturing has happened in your character as a result of the problems you've had to address?*

24. *What spiritual growth has resulted due to your life's problems? Give examples.*

BEYOND SUFFERING INTO GROWTH *(79)*

Sometimes we have a tendency to approach problems as if they are simply an exercise in learning endurance and patience. But go further than merely tolerating bad times. Begin to wonder and be curious. Ask God about your own control issues, about idealized expectations of him and life, about brokenness, selfishness, and the like. When you do, you will often find things to grow from, change, heal, or repent of that can provide new life for you.

25. *Rather than just reading about asking God, ask God right now to use your current problems to reveal to you areas where you need to grow.*

26. *Follow up by asking God—or a trusted and able counselor—to help you outline steps to take toward that growth and then to hold you accountable for taking those steps.*

GOD, HELP ME WELCOME THE PROBLEMS OF LIFE AS GIFTS. LIKE A CHILD, I DON'T LIKE IT WHEN THINGS DON'T GO MY WAY. FORGIVE ME FOR NOT TRUSTING YOU TO KNOW BETTER. FORGIVE ME FOR DECIDING WHAT IS BEST FOR ME. AND PLEASE HELP ME LOOK FORWARD TO THE GOOD THINGS YOU HAVE FOR ME AS YOU GUIDE ME THROUGH PROBLEMS. TEACH ME TO HEAR YOUR VOICE AND MAKE ME WILLING TO FOLLOW YOU. IN JESUS' NAME, AMEN.

TAKING STEPS ALONG THE WAY:
EMBRACING PROBLEMS AS GIFTS

✦ *Where are you on your journey?* Describe your usual response to problems.

✦ *Where do you want to be?* Now explain what you would like your usual response to be—and why.

✦ *What will you do to get there?* Consider what you can do to better appreciate God's sovereign role in your history as well as in world history. Study, too, the lives of believers who have gone before us, and learn from them how to embrace problems as gifts.

FURTHER THOUGHTS

FURTHER THOUGHTS

7

PRINCIPLE SEVEN:
TAKE LIFE AS IT COMES

I (John) have a bone disease called *osteopenia*, meaning that my bones are too porous. Osteopenia, a precursor to the better-known osteoporosis, can lead to easy fracturing and slow healing of the bones. My doctor has me on a regimen built around certain supplements and daily weight-bearing exercises that induce the bones to strengthen themselves. And every year I get a particular set of x-rays taken so the doctor can measure if my condition is improving or deteriorating. Bones change very slowly, so more frequent x-rays are not helpful. To live with these long periods of time with the unknown has taken a little getting used to. *Waiting is difficult.*

1. *When have you lived through a difficult period of waiting?*

2. *Looking back, what benefits came during that waiting period?*

3. *What, if anything, are you waiting for now?*

Waiting is difficult. I have to say, though, that the situation I find myself caught in has offered me some benefits. For one thing, it's showing me so clearly that I am not the master of time. Here is a reality that we would all do well to accept: *When God makes a way for us, that way will generally take time.* Time is the field in which God has chosen to operate to get things done.

Why does God take time? I've witnessed again and again: *Time allows God's healing ingredients to be applied to our situation.* We need thorough and repeated exposure to God's love, truth, grace, and help. We don't generally learn things the first time we hear them. And wounded hearts take time before they're ready or able to make use of the help they are being offered. Time really is a blessing and not a curse.

4. *Think about how an antibiotic works in your body. You take it for an infection over a period of days. With time, the medicine can affect every part of the infected system. Time also allows the antibiotic to interact repeatedly with the infection, so that it is systematically weakened and eventually destroyed. What does that process show you about the importance of time?*

5. *Having read these two paragraphs, think again about your life and identify a situation or two where time really was a blessing.*

But I Want It Now! *(83)*

Letting time pass is not easy. Time often brings out in us that childish part that demands to have things fixed right now. But when we insist on shortcuts and quick fixes we tend to repeat the same problems over and over again, getting nowhere. A helpful way to understand why we need to develop patience is to remember this: *If a goal is meaningful, it will require time.*

6. *What meaningful goal(s) are you working toward now?*

7. *What kind of timeframe do you find yourself dealing with? What is your attitude toward that timing?*

What makes it hard to wait, I believe, is that time has a sort of "underground" nature. By that I mean God is often making a way for us when we cannot even see his hand at work. During that time when it seems nothing is happening on our behalf, it's a gift of faith to be able to trust that God is at work in our relationships, our families, our work, and even in our own hearts.

Consider this parable that Jesus told: "This is what the kingdom of God is like. A man scatters seed on the ground. Night and day, whether he sleeps or gets up, the seed sprouts and grows, though he does not know how. All by itself the soil produces grain—first the stalk, then the head, then the full kernel in the head. As soon as the grain is ripe, he puts the sickle to it because the harvest has come" (Mark 4:26–29).

This story teaches that for God to make a way, we need to undertake two tasks. The first is to *sow whatever seed he gives us.* This might mean admitting a truth, confronting a problem, or giving up something to God that we've been holding onto. Our second task is to *wait without trying to rush God's pace.* He has a task also. He makes a way by taking the ingredients of growth and producing something good in our lives.

8. *When, in retrospect, have you seen that God was at work when nothing seemed to be happening in your life?*

9. *What does your answer to the preceding question suggest to you about the waiting you're doing right now?*

10. *During this season of waiting, what "seed" has God given you to sow? Be specific about the seed and about what you are doing—or could be doing—to sow it.*

11. *What does the task "wait without trying to rush God's pace" mean to you in your current circumstances? Again, be specific.*

If there's any one thing that helps us tolerate time's passage, it is *getting actively involved in the process of development God has us in.* It helps a great deal to become actively engaged in the tasks, experiences, learning, trials, and relationships that are part of his path for us.

TIME ALONE DOES NOT HEAL (86)

By the same token, it's important to know that time's passage is not enough for God to make a way. Many people who believe that time heals all things find themselves stuck in a holding pattern in life. They wait for God to change things, or for another person to come around, or for their feelings to be transformed, and they're disappointed when the change doesn't occur.

12. *Are you waiting for time to take care of things for you? If so, why?*

13. *What is a better option for you than waiting for God to change things, for another person to come around, or for your feelings to be transformed?*

Time is simply a context in which God's healing ingredients interact with your situation. All the other elements that God uses to make a way are still necessary. People don't merely wait for a sprained ankle to heal. They get the brace, do the stretches and physical therapy, and carefully apply heat and massages. Time, by itself, is never enough.

14. *Healing components are love, truth, support, advice, safety, and accountability. What are you doing to surround yourself with all of these components that you need to do the tasks in the way God makes?*

Time alone is often time wasted, while time, with the healing components added, will produce deep and long-lasting results.

EACH SEASON HAS ITS ROLE (86)

Time has some close relatives: We call them *seasons*. Not all periods of time are the same. They have different uses and meanings in God's scheme of things. It helps to understand the nature of the varying seasons, so we can understand our tasks and expectations to help time do its work. As the Bible teaches, "There is a time for everything, and a season for every activity under heaven: a time to be born and a time to die, a time to plant and a time to uproot" (Ecclesiastes 3:1–2).

Here is a way to look at the seasons for growth you will need to use and adapt to in order for God to make a way. They relate to any situation or context of growth and struggle we might be experiencing.

Winter is a time for clearing out dead things, debris, and stones that are in the way of future growth. You mend and repair broken fences and machines. You set up and plan for the future. You might work on getting your schedule and affairs in order to have time and space for your goal. You may research which resources (good churches, groups, experts) you need. Winter lets you settle in and get ready for growth.

Spring is a time of new beginnings and fresh hope. You plow and aerate the soil, providing fertilizer, water, and a controlled climate. In the springtime of your growth, you'll begin to get involved in the plans and commitments you made last winter. When you see initial changes beginning to peek out from the soil, you may need to protect them from people and circumstances that might trample on them and snatch them away.

Summer is the time when growth is very apparent. You're in a maintenance mode, making sure that what was begun in spring continues. In the summertime of your growth, you are diligent to keep going. Don't be lulled into stopping because some good changes began last season. Stay with the program for the full harvest next season. Keep working on the same tasks and the same relationships because you're building on the work God has begun in you.

Fall is the time of harvest when you reap what you have sown! You experience the benefits of the work and spend time picking the fruit, using some today and storing some for the upcoming times of cold and dark. In the fall of personal growth, you see changes in your emotions, behavior, relationships, career, and the like. They are not just cosmetic changes but are truly the product of internal transformation. In that particular area of life you are a new person. So it's a time of celebration and gratitude to God.

15. *In some important area of your life, which season are you in? Explain.*

16. *According to the descriptions above, what are the tasks of that season?*

17. *Now list what you are doing—or would like to do—as you address the tasks of your season. Note, too, who will help you stay on track for doing these tasks.*

We are by nature people who look for four seasons of the fall harvest. We desire results now and are easily disheartened when they do not readily appear. It is not easy to submit to the tasks of the season you're in, but those who adapt will reap in due time. The others will, regretfully, keep making the same mistakes and enduring the same failure and pain.

TAKE HOLD OF THESE GREAT TRUTHS *(88)*

Time and "seasons" are the context in which God makes a way for us. Take hold of the great truths that they teach us. Learn their ways and use them to make something in your life better.

18. *Spend a few minutes looking back over your life. What seasons do you see?*

19. *What fruit resulted from the tasks of winter, spring, and summer?*

20. *What sort of fruit do you hope to celebrate in the next fall of your life?*

We can always be sure that, as we walk through time, doing our part and allowing the seasons of life to work great changes in us, the God who inhabits eternity walks at our side, doing his deeply transforming work. *We are never left on our own!*

GOD, IT'S AMAZING HOW YOU WORK IN THE LIVES OF YOUR PEOPLE. SOMETIMES YOUR WORK IS HIDDEN; SOMETIMES I HAVE TO WAIT A LONG TIME TO SEE WHAT YOU'VE BEEN DOING; AND SOMETIMES YOUR WORK IS OBVIOUS, IMMEDIATE, AND TOTALLY AMAZING. THANK YOU THAT YOU'RE WITH ME THROUGH ALL OF MY WINTERS, SPRINGS, SUMMERS, AND FALLS, AND THAT YOU'RE ALWAYS AT WORK IN ME. THANK YOU THAT YOU'RE THE ONE WHO MAKES GROWTH HAPPEN. IN JESUS' NAME, AMEN.

Taking Steps Along the Way:
Taking Life As It Comes

◆ *Where are you on your journey?* Think again about the season of life you're in and whatever waiting you're doing right now. What blessings of this season, of this period of waiting, can you thank God for and truly enjoy?

◆ *Where do you want to be?* We all like fall, the season of fruitfulness. What fruit do you hope to harvest in the next harvest season of your life?

◆ *What will you do to get there?* Carefully consider the tasks that are yours right now as you anticipate, by God's grace, a harvest celebration. Outline specifically your to-do list for this season and find someone who will be with you in the process. Then be diligent in your work.

FURTHER THOUGHTS

FURTHER THOUGHTS

8

PRINCIPLE EIGHT:
LOVE GOD WITH ALL YOU ARE

Years ago I (John) was on the Sunday service response team in the church I attended. When the pastor preached, he would invite people to come to the front if they needed prayer or spiritual help. One Sunday, Nancy came to the front in tears about an issue involving her teenage son, Scott. The boy was rebellious, doing drugs, and had major problems in school. Every few weeks Nancy came forward again, and finally she asked if we could talk over lunch.

When we met, I saw this single mom's sincere love for God, but I told her I wanted her to think about something: "I think it's possible that you are not loving God enough for him to help you." I explained, "Suppose you have a stomach pain that doesn't go away. You see a doctor who diagnoses you with an irritated stomach lining and puts you on medication. But suppose you forgot to tell him you're allergic to some food you ate last night. Even with the medication you're taking, you would still have stomach pains. You were totally serious and totally committed to getting well, but this particular part of your system—your allergy—was not involved in the treatment. As a consequence, you won't get the results you need. All of you must be present to be healed."

Nancy realized the point of my story and asked, "Which part of me is not showing up in my situation?"

1. *Ask yourself that same question: "Which part of me—that is, what feelings, attitudes, or aspects of my soul—is not showing up in my situation?"*

2. *In light of your answer above, share your ideas about what this means: "It's possible that you are not loving God enough for him to help you."*

When Nancy asked my opinion, I told her that I thought fear was a large part of her life and that it sounded as if she was handling all that fear by herself. "Fear," I explained, "is one thing you don't bring to your relationship with God."

Fortunately, Nancy began facing her fears. She asked God for help with them, and she talked to people who helped her deal with them. In time, her life began changing, as she became less afraid to do what it took to help Scott. As she let God have her fear, he gave her something much better—the renewal of her son.

3. *Now consider what part(s) of your life you are not bringing into your relationship with God. Be specific as you identify them.*

4. *When will you take to God that part (or those parts) of you that he already knows about anyway and that he wants to help you with?*

Let Love Lead *(92)*

God loves you unconditionally and desires to make a way for you through your difficult situation. Finding his way is also a matter of love on your part. Loving God as fully as you can, with every fiber of your being, is the only true and meaningful beginning point. Loving God is so important that Jesus identified it as the first and greatest commandment: "Love the Lord your God with all your heart and with all your soul and with all your mind. This is the first and greatest commandment" (Matthew 22:37–38).

Loving God is the greatest command because it serves as an all-encompassing principle that covers all the other rules of life. If we love God, connect to him, and follow him, we'll end up doing the things that he wants which are best for us. Other rules, principles, and commands are not ignored; rather, they are fulfilled. If you love God, it follows that you will value what he values and see things the way he sees them.

5. *Explain how loving God and loving others as we love ourselves (Matthew 22:37–40) will enable us to obey the following commands:*
   Exodus 20:3
   Matthew 5:44–45
   Matthew 6:19
   Galatians 6:2
   James 1:27

When you are in a bad situation in life and can't find it within yourself to know what the next step should be—*love God.* It's impossible for us to misstep when we begin with that command.

Yet loving God is both simple and complicated. We have been "fearfully and wonderfully made" by God (Psalm 139:14), and we have complex aspects inside ourselves. This is what Jesus was referring to when he talked about our loving God with all our heart, soul, and mind. Every one of us is familiar with the experience of having conflicting feelings, say, about a relationship or about desiring something that conflicts with our values. All of these parts of ourselves—heart, soul, and mind—need God, need him to know them, and need to be loved by him.

6. *Why do we—why do you—hold back parts of ourselves from God?*

7. *Some people are good at loving God with their head but not with their heart. They are good at principles and knowing what's right and prudent to do, but often their heart feels dead or burdened. Or they have strong emotions that are hard to control, no matter what their brain tells them to do. Do you have an easier time loving God with your head or your heart? Why do you think that is? And what will you do to learn to love God more fully, to love him with both your head and heart?*

Our heart, soul, and mind all exist together, connected but separate. They were all designed to love God with all their might. When that happens, they are completely connected to the Source of love and life, and receive all they need.

What's Inside You That God Wants to Love? *(93)*

Here is a brief list of some of the most important aspects of your inner being. These pieces of you all need to be joined to God so that they can take part in helping you find his way.

+ **Values.** Our values make up what is important to us and what is not. What is important to God needs to be important to you. Some core values might be that God is real, that he loves you, and that following him is the most important thing you can do. Our values guide and direct us. When we don't love God with our values—that is, when we don't derive our values from him—we are sure to go astray.

+ **Passions.** Often people are hesitant to let God into their passions. But when you turn your passions over to God, he can transform them into passions that work for and with him. It's good to remember that God is the Author of passion. Allow your love for God to fuel your passions.

+ **Emotions**. God created us with a wide range of emotions, which serve as a signal for us to let us be aware of the state of our soul. Are we afraid and in danger, joyful and feeling loved, at peace, angry, or sad? When we love God with our feelings, positive and negative, he uses them to help us grow and learn about ourselves.

+ **Hurts.** God will make a way when you allow him into the places of your wounds. Remember that he is no stranger to hurt, and he will heal your wounds when you give them to him.

+ **Loves.** Sometimes we love those who are good for us, and sometimes we love those who are not so good for us. When you bring your loves to God, he transforms what we love so that we begin to invest in and trust the right people.

+ **Motives.** Underlying our choices in life are our motives, which are our deeper reasons for our actions. Expose these motives (being caring, responsible, and free; being self-protective, fearful, or selfish) to God so that he can transform them into motives like his own.

+ **Sins.** We harbor sinful thoughts, speak sinful words, and do sinful deeds. When you bring your sins to God, he forgives freely, heals, and provides a way to work through them and find victory and freedom.

+ **Talents.** God designed all of us with strengths and gifts so that we can take part in helping others have a better life. Love God with your talents.

+ **Preferences and opinions.** Don't be afraid to bring to God your unique preferences (a certain kind of church or worship style, certain types of people). He will make a way for you to sort out your preferences and use them to make a better life.

8. *Which of these internal parts of you are you not yet letting God know or love?*

9. *What do you think God will do—in you, for you, and through you—once you give him those parts you just identified? Be specific about each one.*

GOD MAKES A WAY AS WE LOVE HIM IN ALL OUR PARTS *(95)*

Getting to know God in all the ways that are possible is a lifelong and all-encompassing journey. The more aspects of our life and soul we can connect with him, the more God is able to make a way for us, for whatever purposes are ahead. This can be about growth and intimacy, using our talents and gifts, success at work, or service to others. At the same time, loving God with every aspect of our inner being can unlock answers about struggles and heartbreaks too: a parenting problem, a dating relationship, a bad habit, or a faith issue.

The bedrock truth is, *God will make a way for us to the extent that we make a way for him.* That's what loving him completely is all about. It's getting our handcuffs off him and saying, "Do whatever you need to do with whatever part of me needs you." It's saying, as Jesus—who loved God completely—said, "Not my will, but yours be done" (Luke 22:42). But it is not about what loving God does for God. It is what loving God does for us. When we love God with all of ourselves, he has access to all the parts that need his love, grace, and support.

10. *In what way(s) do you have handcuffs on God?*

11. *In what area(s) of your life do you struggle to say to God, "Not my will, but yours be done"?*

12. *Talk to God about these handcuffs and struggles. By doing so, you'll be giving him some access to them and opening yourself to more of his love, grace, and support.*

We are designed to flourish when we connect to and love God. Conversely, we wither away when we're not connected to him (John 15:5). Also, when we love God with all of ourselves, the aspects of our inner beings that connect to God, depend on him, and love him begin to work together in a harmonious unity.

13. *What do these statements suggest about how connected to God you are at the moment?*

14. *What do these statements suggest about what you can do to strengthen that connection?*

God is a healer (Psalm 147:3). And his healing process works to the extent that we bring all of our inner parts to that process. Suppose a person has experienced the loss of a significant long-term relationship with someone she loved deeply. She tries to pray over it, get over it, and think positively, yet the intense feelings of grief remain. Whatever the reason, she avoids bringing to God her need for close human contact. When she realizes this, she understands that God heals to the extent that we love and connect to him. She is then free and able to love God with her need.

15. *What issue are you not fully bringing to God?*

16. *Consider your hesitation in light of the fact that "God heals to the extent that we love and connect to him." When will you love God with your need?*

WE LOVE GOD—BECAUSE GOD *IS* LOVE (97)

God is about love. He makes a way for those who love him with everything they have, with every fiber of their being. You can be sure that the more of yourself you make available to God, the more you can grow, be healed, and find his way. *God will make a way for us to the extent that we make a way for him.*

17. *What obstacle, challenge, or setback are you most concerned about right now?*

18. *Begin to search your heart carefully. Find out if the solution rests in bringing some unknown, unloved, or disconnected piece of your inner self to the light of God's love, care, and healing ability.*

Love God with every part of yourself—heart, soul, and mind—and watch the real miracles of your life begin to unfold.

GOD, YOU WILL MAKE A WAY FOR ME TO THE EXTENT THAT I MAKE A WAY FOR YOU. PLEASE SHOW ME HOW I'M NOT MAKING A WAY FOR YOU. SHOW ME WHAT PARTS OF ME I'M NOT LOVING YOU WITH. AND

SHOW ME THE PARTS OF ME I'M NOT LETTING YOU LOVE. TEACH ME
TO LOVE YOU WITH ALL THAT I AM, WITH ALL MY HEART, WITH ALL
MY MIND, AND WITH ALL MY SOUL. IN JESUS' NAME, AMEN.

TAKING STEPS ALONG THE WAY:
LOVING GOD

◆ *Where are you on your journey?* Identify those parts of you with which you
seem to freely and easily love God—and those parts that you hold back for
whatever reason.

◆ *Where do you want to be?* In your own words, describe the kind of relationship you would like to have with God, who is also your heavenly
Father.

◆ *What will you do to get there?* Look back through this chapter and write
down any ideas you have for what you will do to love God with more of
who you are.

FURTHER THOUGHTS

FURTHER THOUGHTS

9

THE PRINCIPLES AT WORK

Y ou've been learning about eight general principles for walking in God's way, and these principles will work in any situation. In this chapter, however, we want to offer you some additional guidelines for twelve common struggles. For a more thorough discussion of any one area, please see our book, God Will Make a Way *(Integrity, 2002).*

DATING AND NEW ROMANCE *(101)*

1. Prepare to date:

   A. Begin with pursuing God (Matthew 6:25–34) and become the healthiest person you can become.

   B. Get your relationship needs met outside the dating context.

   C. Learn your patterns (old relationship patterns from your original family, seeking completion for something you lack in yourself, idealistic wishes for yourself, inability to set boundaries, fear of closeness or intimacy) and work on them so you do not repeat them.

D. Date according to a few nonnegotiable values (faith, honesty, sexual purity, etc.). Avoid vileness, faithlessness, perversity, slander, evil, pride, deceit, and lying.

E. Expand your tastes. Be open to going out with people who you would normally not have on your list.

F. Be yourself from the beginning. Don't adapt to what you think the other person will like. Be who you are and give the other person the freedom to do the same.

G. Don't put up with bad behavior, and set good boundaries.

H. Take your time. You would not allow a stranger into your house without proper identification, but many people allow virtual strangers into their hearts, minds, souls, and bodies.

I. Stay connected in other relationships. Members of your support system are the ones who are most objective about the people you are dating.

J. Get active. Network with friends and family, pursue the things you enjoy, join others who have the same need, use your gift of hospitality, and do something structured.

K. Look in the mirror. Is something about your personality, behavior, or the way you come across to others getting in the way of meeting people?

L. Keep yourself sexually pure. Honor sex as something holy and keep it confined to the marriage relationship.

2. Abide in God—and have fun! God is the one who will make a way, so walk with him daily. Pray about your dating life and ask him what he wants you to do.

MARRIAGE AND RELATIONSHIPS *(121)*

1. Have a framework that reflects God's purposes:

   A. *Our marriage has God at its center.* Invite him into your relationship and go to him for guidance and direction about your marriage.

   B. *Our marriage is our most important relationship.* Make your spouse your top priority. Remember that what you invest in the most tends to grow the most (Matthew 6:21).

   C. *We are committed to truth without compromise in our marriage* (Colossians 3:9). A marriage is only as strong as the honesty that the partners bring to it.

   D. *We will grow personally in our marriage.* According to God's design, marriage provides us a context in which to mature and grow. Keep in mind that your spouse does not exist to make you happy.

   E. *Our marriage will be lived in community.* Marriage was never designed to be a self-sufficient organism.

2. Respect "I," "you," and "we" in your marriage; be willing to sacrifice "I" for "you" as well as for "we."

3. Develop closeness; work on bringing all of yourselves to each other.

4. Be responsible; have a high sense of ownership for yourself and your marriage.

5. Make friends with the reality of who your spouse truly is.

6. Seek God's path of healing:

   A. Begin with God.

   B. Identify the underlying problem.

   C. Remove the log from your own eye.

   D. Speak the truth lovingly.

   E. Use God's resources.

7. God has reconciled the world to himself (2 Corinthians 5:19), and that reconciliation encompasses the difficulties in your marriage. Seek him and the path that he will show you. It may be a difficult one. Yet he walks it with you—and with your spouse.

INTIMACY AND SEX *(135)*

1. Sexuality reflects the nature and heart of God. It is truly a God thing. Sex is deeply rooted in relationship, as God is.

2. Sex cannot be clearly parsed into either physical or emotional terms. It involves both body and soul.

3. God can make a way whatever problem arises—a problem with desire, arousal, orgasm, addictions, broken trust, etc.

4. A healthy sex life begins with love, and love involves the whole person: heart, soul, mind, and strength.

5. In healthy marriages, both people wholeheartedly take ownership of whatever they are supposed to do.

   A. *Ownership means shared responsibility.* When a wife has to shoulder her husband's load, she will begin to feel like she is married to a child. In turn, he will begin to feel he is married to a parent. When this parent-child dynamic occurs in a marriage, sexual desire and arousal often begin to decrease.

   B. *Ownership means separateness.* Separateness is realizing that while the two in marriage are one flesh, they are still two souls, each of whom must one day give an account of him- or herself before God (2 Corinthians 5:10). Separateness helps each person to assist the other's growth. And separateness creates the longing that is required for sexuality.

   C. *Ownership means self-control.* Self-control has to do with things like having our values dictate our behavior and attitudes as opposed to allowing our impulses, instincts, and appetites to control them. People who are self-controlled make their decisions based on their heart, soul, and mind all coming to a conclusion about something.

6. Acceptance of your spouse means relating lovingly and without judgment to everything about your mate. It is embracing the reality of his or her strengths and weaknesses, gifts, and imperfections.

7. One of the greatest gifts of marriage is that of sex. If you are experiencing difficulties in this wonderful area of life, do not resign yourself to the problem. God has a way. Ask him for the next step.

TOXIC PEOPLE AND CONFLICT *(151)*

1. The degree to which God can make a way for you often depends on how strong a stance you take against the things that destroy the way that he is making. God's way is to stand up against bad things. That is what he does, and it is what he tells us to do as well.

2. God wants us to be very careful to stay clear of people who can destroy the life that he desires to create for us. One of the most spiritual things that anyone can do is to combat toxicity by avoiding it or by con-fronting it.

3. Be prepared to encounter a lot of resistance, arguments, justifications, excuses, attacks, and the like when you are dealing with difficult people.

4. If the person doesn't respond to the initial confrontation, you need to take a stronger stand by giving him or her some consequences. Stand on your values. Do not go forward to participate in evil.

5. Imperfect behavior is not the same as toxic behavior, and it's important to learn to recognize the difference.

6. If you avoid imperfect people and refuse to love them, you will get off the path that God is making for you. Your path will always include imperfect people, just like you and me. Don't be too demanding or judgmental. Yet if a person's behavior toward you is truly destructive, set stronger limits. You are to avoid things that destroy.

CHILDREN AND PARENTING *(167)*

1. Parenting begins with God, the Parent of all of us. And every time you, as a parent, help your children grow in some way, you are preparing them for an eternal walk with God himself.

2. God's purpose is to grow up his kids, and that is the parents' goal as well. Our goal is to create independently functioning adults. In other words, God's design for you as a parent is to be constantly working yourself out of a job.

3. Here are some of the lessons your child needs to learn in order to mature in life:
   A. *Love and connect with others.* God designed us for emotional connection, or bonding, with himself and with others (Psalm 22:9).
   B. *Shoulder the burdens of life.* Train your children to take ownership of their own behavior, life, goals, and problems by giving them love, rules, choices, and consequences.
   C. *Adapt to reality.* This involves experiencing grief, offering forgiveness, and knowing acceptance.

4. Here are some principles to help you be the parent your child needs you to be:
   A. *Stay future-oriented.* When dealing with a child's disobedience or struggle in some area, ask yourself, What can I do about this that will help create a grownup in a few years? When we simply solve the external

symptom, we can be assured that the underlying problem will manifest itself again, in the same form or some other form.

B. *Distinguish between can't and won't* when your child is experiencing difficulty with something. Use wisdom, God's guidance, and the input of others to help.

C. *Keep love and limits together.* Be emotionally connected and strict at the same time. And don't be divided between yourselves, with one being the "loving" parent and the other the "strict" one. This split causes problems for your relationship and for your children.

5. Know that you aren't alone in your parenting. God is always with you. Look to him and his resources. Let him parent you as you parent your kids.

FEAR AND ANXIETY *(183)*

1. Fear is our emotional response to danger; it warns us that something is either happening or about to happen, and when that signal goes off, our entire system calls out the resources.

2. Fear hinders us in some situations:
   A. Bad things truly are happening, but your fear is overwhelming.
   B. You feel alone in the universe, without God.
   C. You feel alone inside, cut off from people.
   D. You have experienced a lack of acceptance.
   E. You have some old baggage.
   F. You have a sense of powerlessness.

G. You have critical voices inside your head.

H. You avoid doing what you fear.

I. You have learned to fear something in particular.

J. You lack certain abilities.

3. If you can identify what specifically is causing your fear, you can go a long way toward finding the cure. Here are some prescriptions, based on the things that cause fear:

A. Fear God and stop the insanity.

B. Get deeply connected with other people.

C. Up the resources to weather the bad things.

D. Overcome alienation by trusting others with your heart.

E. Create structure in your life.

F. Get accepted.

G. Deal with old baggage.

H. Ask God to help you gain a sense of personal power.

I. Find people who are doing what you're afraid to do and learn from them.

J. Make some fear normal. Avoid developing "fear of fear."

K. Evict negative voices and find new ones from God and others.

L. Get back on the horse, gradually. We overcome fear by facing it gradually.

M. Gain new skills.

N. Discover that you can learn by learning.

O. Depend on the Holy Spirit through faith.

P. Seek professional help.

4. "God did not give us a spirit of timidity, but a spirit of power, of love and of self-discipline" (2 Timothy 1:7). So take hold of the Holy Spirit through faith in God and develop that power, love, and self-discipline. When you do, you will find that God is a God who makes a way through fear.

Divorce and Lost Love (203)

1. It's impossible to overstate the damage done by divorce. It permeates every part of your life. It changes your identity. Your friends take sides or get weird. You undergo massive lifestyle changes. And the deepest parts of your soul, where the most precious, fragile, and vulnerable parts of your heart reside, are shattered and torn apart.

2. The depth that you have loved another is the depth to which that person can hurt you. If marriage were not so profound, divorce would not be so devastating.

3. With God's help you can work through the pain and come out on the other end a better, more mature, and more complete person.

4. Become the person God wants you to be. You can develop and grow into the individual who God created you to be and have the opportunity to discover the richness of life apart from marriage.

5. Embrace grief. Accept the reality of what is; remember and experience value for the loved one. Let go of the desire to see only the bad, and allow yourself to appreciate and let go of the good person you are leaving. This is the key to freedom beyond grief in divorce.

6. Take stock of your contributions. Ensure that you grow past the mistakes of the past (withdrawal of love, control, unloving criticism, irresponsibility, passivity, deception, moral superiority, codependency) and do not recreate them in the future.

7. Know when to date again. Wait. Develop a long-term and stable relationship with God. Get connected to a community of healthy, loving, and honest people.

8. God is the God of fresh starts. Go to him with your past and your present, and ask him to show you the way to a life of renewal (1 Peter 5:10–11).

BAD HABITS AND ADDICTIONS *(217)*

1. Addiction is an inability to stop a repeated and compulsive use of an activity, behavior, or substance in spite of negative consequences.

2. In general, most addicts follow this two-step path: They begin with a behavior that brings them pleasure. Then they become psychologically or physically dependent on the behavior or substance.

3. Addiction becomes apparent when a person doesn't acknowledge the negative consequence, explains it away, or acknowledges it and yet is unable to stop.

4. Be honest with yourself about whether you might be addicted.
   A. Has something in your life gotten control of you?
   B. Are you unwilling or unable to give up that behavior despite its negative consequences?
   C. Do you go through periods of withdrawal?
   D. Do you obsess about the behavior more and more?
   E. Do you often feel guilty or ashamed of the behavior and yet find that you are unable to stop?
   F. Have others noticed the effects of the behavior?
   G. Do you feel better when engaged in the behavior and then find that other things in life cannot bring you the same degree of pleasure, excitement, involvement, or momentary relief that the behavior does?
   H. Have you lost consciousness or memory because of a substance? Do you try to cover up what you do?

5. An addicted person needs to learn to admit that she is powerless over her addiction and totally helpless to stop. She needs to lean on God as a source of power in the addiction itself.

6. It does not matter what you are addicted to. It does not matter how long you have been addicted. It does not matter how severe the consequences. If you are willing to allow God to make a way, he will. All you have to do

is stop trying to tell yourself to be strong, admit that you are weak, and get into his system of recovery.

DISCOURAGEMENT AND DEPRESSION *(233)*

1. God makes a way through depression (Psalm 18:28).

2. Depression includes these symptoms: a depressed mood, changes in appetite, changes in sleep patterns, fatigue, self-image distortions, problems in concentration, and hopeless feelings.

3. Depression is the soul's cry for help, and in this sense it is a blessing.

4. No matter what is causing or driving your depression, in order for the depression to lead to life, you need relationship. Reach out to God and his people with whatever you have the ability to reach out with—your need, your commitment, your pain, or your awareness.

5. Ask God to help you identify the cause of your depression. Ask him to open windows inside you to help you find out what is true about you: inability to grieve losses, lack of ability to need and depend on others emotionally, problems in responsibility and freedom, burnout, perfectionism, feelings of self-condemnation, unresolved trauma, and/or medical causes.

6. Depression can be debilitating and frightening. However, God is right there with you in the black hole as he fills it up with love and light, and provides a way out, back into his world. Trust him for that.

GUILT AND SHAME *(247)*

1. One of the reasons we feel guilty in life is simply this: We are guilty (Romans 3:23). Every human is born with a capacity for knowing that there are standards in the universe and that we do not always live up to those standards.

2. We respond to our guilt in different ways. Some people try to get away from it, others try to rewrite what they've been taught about right and wrong, and still others live with their guilt and take on the identity of a "sinner." Some give up the standard altogether, and others try to medicate the guilt.

3. Everyone has blown it, and everyone can be forgiven by just believing in God (Romans 3:21–24).

4. You not only have to learn about forgiveness, you have to experience it. You do that by bringing your faults out into the light, confessing them to other people who are safe and loving, and then experiencing the love and forgiveness that they offer you in the name of God.

5. All of us struggle. The Bible shows us how God makes a way out of our perfectionism—he just nukes it. If we could see ourselves as imperfect, as he does, we would become humble and be a lot more comfortable accepting ourselves.

6. Jesus taught that our spiritual relationship with God is intertwined with our relationships with each other.

7. Confession allows you to receive a person's forgiveness. You will be relieved of unnecessary suffering. You will find resolution even if the other person does not forgive you.

8. God addresses the reality of the problem and wants us to work on it, wants us to feel sorry, instead of feeling guilty about it. Guilt is all about me and how bad I am when I sin, and remorse is all about you and the effects of my sin on you. Feeling guilty will never motivate you to lasting change.

9. Children feel guilty when they fall short of their parents' standards. Since God has told us that he forgives us for not living up to his standard, we are free to "grow up" and be adults for the first time.

10. Get on this path to freedom.
    A. Turn to God and ask him for forgiveness (1 John 1:9).
    B. Look at the reality of your failure and take it seriously. That is called repentance.

C. If you have hurt others, go to them (unless it would be somehow destructive), ask for forgiveness, and be reconciled (Matthew 5:23–24).

D. Confess your failures (all of them) to another person who understands God's forgiveness and will administer it to you (James 5:16).

E. Work to make the false standards and messages in your head more realistic (Ecclesiastes 7:20).

F. Get in community with other people.

G. Do an entire moral inventory of your life, confess your sin to God, ask for forgiveness, and share your sin with someone safe.

H. When you have accusing voices in your head about your failures, remember that they are lies (Romans 8:1).

I. Memorize Scripture about forgiveness.

11. Jesus forgives everything for those who ask. So ask him and believe what he promises: He will forgive. Then act like the innocent person that you now are!

WEIGHT LOSS AND HEALTH *(263)*

1. All issues are spiritual issues, and all struggles are spiritual struggles.

2. God is present and involved in all aspects of our lives. God cares about weight issues, he is present with you, and he has a way for you.

3. God's grace—his unmerited favor—is a key factor in weight control. When God favors you, it means he is on your side; he wants your best. So go to

God, surrender your willpower and attempts to try harder, and take the humble step of admitting you are powerless in your own strength.

4. That which is seen reflects that which is unseen: The body can reflect the state of the soul. Weight issues are often symptoms of something going on inside: a problem, a lack, or a brokenness. Ask yourself, *What could my weight be telling me about the state of my soul?*

5. Consider whether any of the following underlying problems could be the cause of your struggle with weight:
    A. You have a deficit or emptiness inside.
    B. You have control deficits or boundary problems.
    C. You hate yourself and eat to medicate the pain.
    D. You have a sense of entitlement.
    E. You are uncomfortable with your sexuality.

6. Enter the life of God. Begin the process of loving him with all your heart, soul, mind, and strength (Mark 12:30). Bring yourself into his ways and allow God to be God in all of your life.

7. People who have sustaining, supportive relationships tend to lose more weight, and keep it off for longer periods, than those who don't (see Ecclesiastes 4:9–10). So ask your friends to support and encourage you as you seek God's way for you in the area of weight control.

8. Find a safe structure (a weight-loss group, an individual counselor, a regular exercise routine).

9. Learn to experience your relationship with God as a pleasant one and food as a pleasant, enjoyable gift rather than a problem.

10. The more reality-based your body image, the better equipped you are to deal with it. God can help you see and experience your body as it really is—not better or worse.

11. Take ownership of the problem. Let go of blame, learn from the past, and take ownership in the present.

PERSONAL GOALS AND DREAMS *(279)*

1. Success comes from following God's laws and from receiving his favor.

2. Although working in the ways that God has ordained does not guarantee our "success," if we don't follow his ways we most likely won't achieve success.

3. Start with God. Trusting God with your goals means believing that he is the source of all good things and that he can instruct you about what is good.

4. If God is your primary goal, then you will reach your other goals, for he will guide you in determining what they are and reaching them.

5. To reach your goals, say "yes" to who you are and "no" to others' definitions and expectations of you.

6. Sometimes it is just not God's will that we reach a particular goal. Yet it is not his will that you never reach any of your goals. If that seems to be happening, the reason may be patterning.

7. See if you can relate to any of these patterns: no defined goals; specific goals, but too unrealistic; specific goals, but underresourced or under-planned; external motivation or definition; derailed by personal weaknesses; start but don't complete or finish; lack of discipline or structure; hit obstacles and not able to recover; failure did you in; people did you in.

8. Identify your strengths and gifts, and operate within them.

9. Before you set out to reach your goals, sit down and figure out what it is going to cost you in terms of money, time, sacrifices, relationships, acquiring skills, emotion, and gaining knowledge.

10. As you count the cost, keep reality in mind. Look at your goals in terms of reality, and let reality motivate you. (If you don't like what you see, you may be more willing to do whatever it takes to change reality.) Also look hard at what will be true if you do not pursue your goals and dreams. (Can you live with that?)

11. Write out a plan.

12. Make little choices. Goals are reached in little steps.

13. Expect challenges and problems, and let these obstacles (fear and other difficult feelings, conflicts with people, failure, lack of resources, lack of abilities, discouragement, doubt, distance from God, second-guessing, and criticism) help you grow.

14. Failure is not the worst thing that can happen to us. Wasting our lives by not trying is.

15. Ask God to show you who you are and what you are to do—and then trust him to make a way.

FURTHER THOUGHTS

FURTHER THOUGHTS

10

CONCLUSION:
BEGIN YOUR JOURNEY TODAY

God's way always works. When you are at some crossroads in life, *when you don't know what to do, God does.* His grace, his leading, and his principles never fail, for he himself cannot fail in his purposes for us: "Do not be afraid or discouraged, for the LORD God, my God is with you. He will not fail you or forsake you" (1 Chronicles 28:20). His way may not always be the same as the one we would have imagined, but it will ultimately be the best way for us.

God's way is not always the easiest way, and often it is not the way we are familiar with. It involves admitting we are powerless and in need, walking in faith, taking risks, and being able to face the truth. Yet his way is truly the only way that helps and heals us. And throughout the ages God has made a way for his people—a way that is based on his nature, his resources, and his Word, which are eternal and never change. Today is no different. God lives and moves among us as he always has, transforming those who earnestly seek his way.

1. *Highlight those statements above that are most encouraging to you.*

2. *What challenge is God issuing you through these two paragraphs?*

In order to help you develop your own vision for what God can do in your life, we want to take you step by step through Beth's journey. She, like you, wanted a better life, and she entered the process of growth we have been describing in this workbook. Over time God changed her—and her life—in ways she had never even imagined. As you read Beth's story, ask God to show you how you can implement these principles so they can begin working for you today, tomorrow, and for the rest of your life.

As we follow Beth's life and choices, we will note which of the principles she was following at each point. They appear as they occurred in her life. Understand that God's way is for *all* of these principles to be at work in our lives. When all are present, we begin to see true and meaningful change. Just as we need to take all the correct medicines for an illness, we need to make sure that we are utilizing all parts of the way of God.

TOO LITTLE, TOO LATE *(298)*

When I (John) met her, Beth's marriage to Don was almost dead. They were involved in an ineffective dance, and their marriage was severely ailing. Finally, Don's affair came to light, and that's when they called me for counseling. We had sessions for a while, but it was too little, too late. Though Beth did everything she could to hold on to the marriage, Don finally admitted that by the time they started counseling, he had already decided to leave. He had agreed to seek help only in order to mollify Beth. Don divorced her and ultimately married the woman with whom he'd had the affair.

Beth had really wanted the marriage to work. The covenant and institution of marriage was very important and sacred to her. Don's decision to get a divorce devastated Beth, and she continued to make attempts to reconcile with him up until he remarried. She humbled herself and let him know she wanted things to work out between them.

This was an early indication of Beth's character, and it offered great promise for future growth and healing by God. Beth never resorted to the usual position of the law: *If you don't want me, I don't want you.* She wanted reconciliation and the restoration of love. Because of this attitude of love over law, I knew that, whatever happened between Beth and Don, ultimately she would put her feet on God's path, and she would be okay. This proved to be true.

BEGINNING A JOURNEY WITH GOD *(300)*

Beth's story is not about her counseling. Therapy was only one piece of the puzzle for her; Beth did many other things to allow God to make a way for her. She came to see God's role as the Source and Designer of life and began depending on him and incorporating his designs into her values and behaviors. *Her journey with God had begun.*

When Beth lost what she wanted most (her marriage), her world crumbled. This loss created room in her heart for God. Beth was beginning to grasp the truth of Jesus' words: "For whoever wants to save his life will lose it, but whoever loses his life for me will find it" (Matthew 16:25). For the first time in her life, she began to understand that having a good marriage was not the most important thing in life. As she discovered a hunger and thirst for God, Beth came to the conclusion that even if God meant for her to be single for the rest of her days, that was preferable to being married if this wasn't his plan for her. In other words, Beth placed God's ways over her desire for marriage.

3. *At what point in your life would you say that your journey with God began?*

4. *What loss in your life has created room in your heart for God?*

5. *What desire have you released to God, wanting even more of what he wants for you? Or what desire do you need to release to him?*

Beth also realized that the surest way to a rich life was to follow God's path. As a result of this new insight, Beth began to bring God from the periphery of her life into the center. She developed a regular devotional life and started reading and studying the Bible, something she enjoyed and began to depend on for insight about her choices and decisions.

6. *What do you do—or could you do—to keep God at the center of your life?*

7. *Where do you go for input regarding choices and decisions you need to make?*

8. *What choices and/or decisions do you currently face? To whom are you turning for perspective, counsel, and perhaps even accountability?*

CHOOSING WISE TRAVELING COMPANIONS *(301)*

As her love for God grew, Beth found a healthy church in which she explored the areas of worship, community, and service. She met some good people of faith, but despite their care for her, they had no knowledge of what struggle, heartbreak, and dysfunction were about. One day when Beth was sad and depressed over losing Don, a woman told her, "Those feelings have no place in faith. You have the victory in Christ, so replace your emotions with victorious emotions." This woman didn't understand that while we do have the victory in Christ, there are still painful battles going on in our lives.

9. *What would you say to the woman who spoke to Beth?*

10. *What battles are going on in your life?*

11. *Why do these battles rage despite Christ's victory over sin and suffering?*

12. *What hope does Christ's victory give you in the midst of your battles?*

Despite some people's inability to relate to what she'd been through and was going through, Beth did not give up. She continued to search for a balanced and healthy support network. She finally developed some close relationships with people who, while certainly not perfect, loved God, each other, and her, and they understood brokenness. She began to open up to them, and they to her. Beth had found her *traveling companions.* They gave her the freedom and motivation to keep on growing.

13. *Who are your traveling companions? Who understands the battles you face?*

14. *Where did you meet these people—or where might you go to meet them?*

15. *What do these traveling companions do that gives you "the freedom and motivation to keep on growing"? What do they do to keep you accountable for taking steps of growth?*

Loving God with All Her Heart *(302)*

Beth literally started to *love God with all her heart, soul, mind, and strength.* All, not just part, of her began to love and follow him. Parts of her that she had not let God handle began coming into a relationship with him. For example, she was able to be honest with God about her anger toward him about the divorce. She also began to bring her dreams and goals in life to God and to let him work on them. Bit by bit, Beth began to love God with all of herself. In turn, God put her life together for her.

16. *What parts of you are you not letting God handle? What anger? What goals and dreams?*

17. *When, if ever, have you consciously released a part of yourself to God for the first time? What did he do with that part of you?*

18. *What about Beth's story encourages you personally?*

OWNING HER FAULTS AND WEAKNESSES *(302)*

In the early weeks after her divorce, Beth worked on sorting out what had happened in the relationship—what was her fault and what was Don's. Her blame initially helped her identify who had done what, so that she could clarify what to work on in herself and what she needed to forgive in Don. Yet Beth continued to talk about Don's failures. I gently confronted her: "Until you are more concerned about your part in what went wrong with your marriage than you are about Don's, you will always be in jail emotionally to this divorce." Beth saw that she had been blaming Don in order to avoid taking ownership of their problems. When she admitted what she had been doing, she stopped blaming him and began shouldering the burden of her own contributions.

19. *To whom, if anyone, are you "in jail emotionally"?*

20. *Who are you blaming for things instead of taking ownership of your problems?*

21. *Why would you be reluctant to shoulder the burden of your own contributions to those problems?*

As she began *owning her faults and weaknesses,* Beth began to see that she had been afraid to confront Don about things and that she had let them go as a result. She had also let him control things because she had been afraid of making mistakes. She had lost her heart and life in the marriage, allowing the marriage to be about only her husband, rather than about both of them. As she began to take owner-ship in her life, she started to work on her fears of rejection and intimacy and began experiencing life, instead of just surviving or existing. She began to risk being emotionally vulnerable with her friends in her support network, and she began to depend on them for love and understanding.

22. *Whether you're married or single, what can you learn from Beth's experience?*

EMBRACING PROBLEMS AS GIFTS *(303)*

At about the same time that God began to do surgery on her heart about taking ownership of her faults, Beth also began *embracing her problems as gifts.* She started to see that despite all the heartache and pain that she had been going through over her divorce, she was learning valuable lessons.

23. *What valuable lesson(s) have you learned as a result of heartache, pain, loss, or difficulty?*

24. *What can you learn from one of your present challenges? Put differently, what lesson do you think God might want to teach you through one of your current struggles? Humbly ask God to speak to you (1 Samuel 3:9).*

God showed Beth things about himself and his love for her that she had not expected. She learned about grace, faith, trust, honesty, patience, and responsibility, and she finally realized that though Don had done evil to her, and she herself had done her share of evil, "God intended it for good" (Genesis 50:20). Beth knew that she had really grown when she realized that she felt gratitude for what she had learned in the ordeal. She might never have learned the important lessons she was learning or made the changes she had made, had it not been for her divorce. As she saw the gifts God had given her through what she had been through, gratitude gradually replaced the bitterness and hurt she had felt for so long.

25. *What aspects of Beth's experience, if any, have you also experienced?*

26. *What aspects of this phase of Beth's journey offer you hope?*

LEAVING BAGGAGE BEHIND *(304)*

Then there was the *baggage to leave behind,* let go of, and forgive—and there was more than Beth had realized. She had been holding on to what had been instead of letting go and moving on to a new existence. In order to move forward, she had a lot of forgiving to do. Yet Beth was determined not to let baggage from the past hinder her present and future life with God, so she continued to accept reality as it was and let go of what she could not have. Beth had grown to the point that she was much more invested in what God and she were up to in the here and now than she was in the past.

27. *What aspect(s) of the past are you holding onto instead of letting go and moving on to a new existence?*

28. *What forgiving do you have to do so you can move forward?*

29. *Beth worked on accepting reality and letting go of what she could not have. What do you need to let go of and what details about your present reality as it is do you need to accept?*

PLACING A HIGH VALUE ON WISDOM *(305)*

Beth had no investment in appearing to have it together. She knew what she didn't know, and she wanted to know what she needed to know. Beth was a learner, and she was very motivated to *place a high value on wisdom.* She understood the clarity and guidance that information brings to people.

30. *In what ways, if any, is your desire to appear to have your act together keeping you from learning and growing? Why is that appearance so important to you?*

31. *Beth wanted the skill in living that comes with wisdom. She lived out this verse from Proverbs: "Get wisdom, get understanding; do not forget my words or swerve from them. Do not forsake wisdom, and she will protect you; love her, and she will watch over you. Wisdom is supreme; therefore get wisdom. Though it cost all you have, get understanding" (4:5–7). What are you doing —or could you do—to "get wisdom"?*

One of the side benefits of Beth's quest for wisdom is that she herself has had much to offer people who are hurting not only from divorce but on a much broader level. Using the wisdom she sought and made part of herself, Beth is now helping others move into personal, emotional, and spiritual maturity.

Taking Life As It Comes *(306)*

Beth naturally placed a value on wisdom, but she had difficulty with the idea of *taking life as it comes*. An accountant, she saw life in pretty straight lines (A leading directly to B), and it did not make sense to her that there would be times of long waiting, periods of regression and failure, and then a season of harvesting and good fruit.

And though she placed the prospect of remarriage into God's hands, she thought she was ready a long time before God did. So she had a few relational shipwrecks. After each failure, however, Beth went back to the drawing board of God, her friends, and the principles. Each time she did, she learned and grew a little more. She sowed more grace, love, and truth into her heart from her resources, and allowed herself to have another season of growth.

32. *What do you appreciate about the example Beth offers you?*

33. *What do you do—or could you do—to sow more grace, love, and truth into your heart?*

Finally, much later than Beth would have ever accepted when she was a control freak, she met Carl. He was the right guy, she was the right girl, and it was the right time. Carl was just as much into God's ways as Beth was. He appreciated the work she had done on herself and had been actively growing himself. They are now happily married and have children of their own, and they are busy helping others find God's way for them.

God made a way for Beth. She did not receive her first heart's desire (Don never returned to her), but she submitted her heart and soul to God's plan and path. Because she did, she not only got a new life in God, she got a second chance at a good marriage. God's work has borne fruit in his time.

34. *Have you submitted your heart and soul to God's plan and path? If not, why not?*

35. *What new life in God are you aware of experiencing since you started exploring and applying the principles of God's way?*

As You Enter God's Way for You *(307)*

We hope you have been encouraged by Beth's story, even if your own journey isn't about marriage. Whatever your journey (whether it concerns your family, a habit or addiction, your career, or your kids), God will make a way for you, as he did for Beth, if you are willing to step out and live according to the principles in this personal discovery guide.

36. *What did you find most encouraging about Beth's story?*

37. *Are you willing to "step out and live according to the principles in this guide"? If not, why not? What kind of support do you need—and where will you go to find such support and accountability?*

God will make a way for you. You may not receive your first desire . . . or you may. That is up to God and what is best for you. At any rate, these eight concepts work because the One who makes a way for us designed them, and he will accomplish his purposes in you as you allow him to.

God bless you and keep you, as you enter the way that he has for you. We want to encourage you, in the words of the apostle Paul, that we are confident "that he who began a good work in you will carry it on to completion until the day of Christ Jesus" (Philippians 1:6).

GOD, THANKS FOR TEACHING ME ABOUT THESE EIGHT IMPORTANT PRINCIPLES OF THE WAY. AND THANK YOU FOR THE ENCOURAGING STORIES ABOUT HOW YOU HEAL AND GUIDE PEOPLE WHO ARE IN A BAD PLACE. THANK YOU, TOO, FOR BEGINNING A GOOD WORK IN ME AND PROMISING TO "CARRY IT ON TO COMPLETION." IN JESUS' NAME, AMEN.

FURTHER THOUGHTS

FURTHER THOUGHTS

FURTHER THOUGHTS

Embark on a Life-Changing Journey of Personal and Spiritual Growth

DR. HENRY CLOUD

DR. JOHN TOWNSEND

Dr. Henry Cloud and Dr. John Townsend have been bringing hope and healing to millions for over two decades. They have helped people everywhere discover solutions to life's most difficult personal and relational challenges. Their material provides solid, practical answers and offers guidance in such areas as *marriage, parenting, dating* and *personal growth*. Each week Dr. Cloud and Dr. Townsend host a unique event called **Monday Night Solutions** in Southern California. They deliver a powerful message of God's love and truth on a wide variety of topics. These compassionate and often humorous presentations are recorded and comprise their extensive audio library. For a complete list of all their books, videos, audio tapes and small group resources, visit:

www.cloudtownsend.com or

800-676-HOPE (4673)

ALSO AVAILABLE from Cloud-Townsend Resources

Dr. Townsend has been conducting popular and life-changing seminars for many years on a wide variety of topics such as *Boundaries in Marriage, Boundaries with Kids, Safe People, Hiding From Love, How People Grow* and *God Will Make a Way*. For information on scheduling a seminar or becoming a seminar partner call **800-676-HOPE (4673)**.

Cloud-Townsend Resources
Solutions for Life
www.cloudtownsend.com